CREATIVE PRODUCT DESIGN

A PRACTICAL GUIDE TO REQUIREMENTS CAPTURE MANAGEMENT

CREATIVE PRODUCT DESIGN

A PRACTICAL GUIDE TO REQUIREMENTS CAPTURE MANAGEMENT

Margaret Bruce and Rachel Cooper

JOHN WILEY & SONS, LTD
Chichester • New York • Weinheim • Brisbane • Singapore • Toronto

Copyright © 2000 by John Wiley & Sons, Ltd,
Baffins Lane, Chichester,
West Sussex PO19 1UD, England

National 01243 779777
International (+44) 1243 779777
e-mail (for orders and customer service enquiries): cs-books@wiley.co.uk
Visit our Home Page on http://www.wiley.co.uk
or http://www.wiley.com

Other Wiley Editorial Offices

John Wiley & Sons, Inc., 605 Third Avenue,
New York, NY 10158-0012, USA

WILEY-VCH GmbH, Pappelallee 3,
D-69469 Weinheim, Germany

Jacaranda Wiley Ltd, 33 Park Road, Milton,
Queensland 4064, Australia

John Wiley & Sons (Asia) Pte Ltd, 2 Clementi Loop #02-01,
Jin Xing Distripark, Singapore 129809

John Wiley & Sons (Canada) Ltd, 22 Worcester Road,
Rexdale, Ontario M9W 1L1, Canada

British Library Cataloguing in Publication Data
A catalogue record for this book is available from the British Library

ISBN 0-471-98720-4

Typeset in 10/12pt Helvetica by C.K.M. Typesetting, Salisbury, Wiltshire
Printed and bound in Great Britain by Biddles Ltd, Guildford and King's Lynn
This book is printed on acid-free paper responsibly manufactured from sustainable
forestry, in which at least two trees are planted for each one used for paper production.

Dedication

Stephen Glennon, Ivan and Joyce Bruce, Cary, Laura and Sarah Cooper

CONTENTS

ACKNOWLEDGEMENTS

EPSRC for supporting the two-year research programme of Requirements Capture. Andrew Wootton and Barny Morris were research assistants on the programme and Alison Roberts was a Post-Graduate Research Student. Liz Barnes, post-graduate researcher, for her input. Jeremy Grammer, Director of Business Processes at GPT and currently Vice-President of Performance Management at Marconi Communications for his interest in the project. Claire Plimmer and Karen Weller at John Wiley and Sons Ltd, for their patience and support. Pauline Brooke for her help and support in compiling the book.

INTRODUCTION

Innovation management and product development is increasingly important for all kinds of businesses. Internet retail and e-commerce has precipitated the emergence of new Internet products and brought into being new ways of banking, shopping and working. Technological advances and consumer expectations are driving change. In the fashion industry, new fibres and fabrics are constantly available and more casual dress in the workplace is fuelling innovation in workwear. Companies have to find ways to manage product development and innovation to enable them to identify new technological advances early and bring these to the consumer more quickly and cheaply than can their competitors. This demands a review of their management of product development activities. Such a review is reinforced by the fact that nearly 50% of product development costs are likely to result in a failed product. In some sectors, such as fast-moving consumer goods (FMCG), the failure rate is 75%. Improvements to innovation management are needed.

Lack of creative ideas is hindering the development of exciting and attractive products in UK business and consumer markets. This statement denotes the situation in the UK, but is a symptom, rather than an explanation, of this. Typically, large companies have product development processes and project management tools and techniques for innovation management. But idea generation and creativity management are not considered to be a problem. Often, corporate product development processes do not take adequate account of the predevelopment phase or the front end of the product development process; new product development processes often start at concept stage missing completely the front end. If it is considered at all it is treated as a phase or stage that products have to go through before the real effort in developing the product begins. For household textiles, the generation of ideas and creative design is given two weeks of effort out of a nine-month cycle. Creative leadership is a skill that effective managers are assumed to possess. Staff recruitment to build up creative teams is not taken seriously. Mavericks are tolerated, or leave, unless they can find a way to work within the corporate culture to channel their creative energies.

As more and more companies have become leaner and outsource expertise, so product development occurs between collaborating companies and also in the supply chain. But the product development management in this context has not been explored.[1] What role do suppliers and distributors take? What role *can* they take? What about customer expectations, and other important stakeholders? If customers fail to be attracted to the product, then it will be unsuccessful.

Requirements capture (RC) is the process by which the needs, preferences and requirements of individuals and groups – stakeholders – significant to product development are researched and identified. Requirements capture defines:

- customer, user and market requirements;
- design requirements; and
- technical requirements.

Defining a process of RC at the front end or predevelopment of the product development process is imperative. The front end is a critical phase because once the concept has been defined, then about 80 per cent of subsequent costs will have been committed. Without a thorough RC process, false assumptions regarding customer, technical and other requirements may be made. Such false assumptions lead to errors in the product specification, which may only be uncovered later in the process. This impacts on time and cost – the later this occurs in the product lifecycle, then the greater the impact. With the current focus on achieving quick response, managers worry that more effort expended on RC at the front end will increase the time of product development. However, companies with intense front-end activities spend 40 per cent less time on product development, than those that ignore this stage. In addition, companies with an effective RC process gain more profits and revenue from new products, than do those that do not have an adequate RC process (Page and Stovall, 1994). Cooper and Kleinschmidt (1988) found that successful new product development was linked directly to investment in front-end activities. The ability to capture and define requirements is linked to critical factors of product development, namely:

---

[1] Innovation management and product development are used interchangeably. Differences between radical and incremental innovations exist, but the management processes entailed are similar.

- time
- cost
- ability to meet customer needs and expectations.

By gaining knowledge of the market environment, technology drivers and the emerging needs of the target market, an understanding will be gained of the tangible and intangible aspects of how the market defines value, all of which are essential in achieving the right product specification. Inherent to RC is risk minimization – gathering, analysing and understanding to optimize the chances of successful product development. RC is a means of ensuring that early on in the product development process, the foundations for the product specification are solid. A well-managed RC process enables:

- definition of product objectives at an early stage; and
- companies to develop the skills they need to exploit emerging market and technological opportunities.

RC management identifies the key stakeholders (suppliers, customers, distributors, designers, engineers, marketing, sales, etc.) in the product development process. RC has to be considered within the innovating company or group of collaborators and within the supply chain. It is a way of planning the process to try to pre-empt difficulties and problems at a later date that could lead to the abortion of the product, or add to development costs, or delay commercialization.

Requirements management is needed throughout the innovation management process. Ideas can change during this process and modifications may be needed. Rather than carrying out changes in an ad hoc fashion, they should be referred back to the original objectives of the project and modifications made systematically.

Model of Requirements Capture

Essentially, three different phases constitute a model of RC. These are shown in Figure 1.1:

- information gathering
- information transformation
- requirements generation.

Acquisition

Acquisition of information, consensus, decision and transformation of this form the main elements of the process of RC. Requirements are at the heart

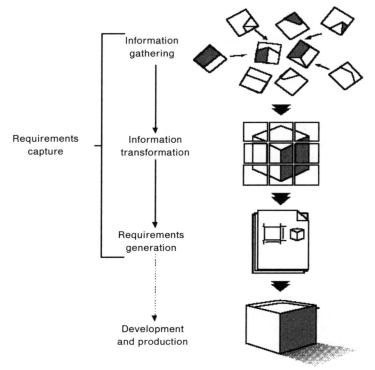

Figure 1.1   Requirements capture

of all product and service concepts. Knowledge enters and exits a firm in many guises (e.g. research reports, individual experiences, gossip, customer feedback etc.) and from many different sources. The output of these sources may be information, data, requirements, opinions, tacit knowledge, ideas etc. Acquisition of requirements knowledge is an ongoing process.

Firms are able to make choices concerning from whom (i.e. the origin of requirements knowledge) and in what format (library, book, report, conversation etc.) requirements knowledge is acquired. However, facilitating soft processes such as relationships and serendipity mean that requirements knowledge will be acquired concurrently with any deliberate and purposeful research process. According to each individual, more or less value will be attached both to the origins of the requirements knowledge and the requirements knowledge itself. Reaching consensus about the requirements may be difficult; some individuals may favour data from formal research reports, whilst others place more credibility on what is discussed in a face-to-face situation. An individual's position in the organization (both formal, social and political) will affect how that consensus is reached.

Focusing on a particular source of requirements knowledge may skew the product specification in favour of one particular origin of requirements knowledge. For instance, the product may be biased to the agenda of engineering (leading to a product that is difficult to sell) or the customer (leading to a product that is costly to manufacture), or a distributor (leading to a product that may provide little or no margin of profit to the supplier).

Knowing whether requirements knowledge is significant may be the responsibility of only a few key individuals based on their experience, judgement and gut feelings in the initial stages. However, the significance of requirements knowledge may also be mediated within a group setting, particularly when individuals (in a team for instance) are learning for the first time about a product or market area. To summarize, five principles of the acquisition activity can be identified:

1. **Identifying origins of requirements knowledge** – firms must be able to identify the origins of requirements knowledge.
2. **Placing significance on requirements knowledge** – firms must identify what level of significance should be placed on the origin of requirements knowledge and the requirements knowledge itself.
3. **Detecting changes in the nature of requirements knowledge** – firms must possess adequate *monitoring* mechanisms that flag up the possibility that changes are taking place in the nature of requirements knowledge, for instance, the changing customer requirements that may alter the core assumptions concerning a product or service.
4. **Tracking and mapping the usage of requirements knowledge** – firms should *record* what requirements knowledge has been used, who acquired it, when it was acquired and the origin of the requirements knowledge.
5. **Maintaining access to requirements knowledge** – once firms have identified the origins of requirements knowledge (whether internal or external) they should ensure that they remain within the boundaries of the firm (if so desired). Who can access requirements knowledge (and how) will have to be decided by the firm.

Information Transformation

This part of the process is the activity whereby meaning is assigned to the information gathered, thereby transforming it into knowledge. Although this is the second activity in the process, it may take place concurrently with information gathering, i.e. meaning is assigned to information the moment it is received from the data source. For example, in a face-to-face interview, a customer answers the question 'What colour car do you prefer?' with 'Red'. The interviewer may immediately assign to the customer's preference a number of meanings, such as red vehicles are more sporty; or red cars are easier to see and therefore safer; or red cars retain their value better. In this way, the original information from the data source is transformed and, in the interviewer's mind, becomes the knowledge that the customer is concerned about the image and styling of cars, or safety issues relating to visibility, or the resale value.

The transformation activity may also continue after the information has been gathered. For instance, when two or more individuals interact, discussing and debating the meaning of information. This interaction may occur informally, for example in discussion with friends or colleagues, or formally, as when individuals are brought together specifically to work on a development project. In this group setting, such soft factors as group dynamics, strength of character or seniority may affect what meaning is collectively assigned to data. Other factors including the social and political environment of the group as well as the wider culture of the company will also affect the outcome.

Three principles of the transformation activity can be defined:

1. **Identification of significant new and existing transformation mechanisms** – firms need to identify and attach significance to those mechanisms that allow them to translate successfully requirements knowledge into products and services. This may include, for instance, the strategic planning department, the engineering manager, the product strategy team, marketing's relationships with lead users, collaboration with external firms, university research departments, etc.

2. **The development of new and existing transformation mechanisms** – knowing which mechanisms are more useful than others will allow firms to focus their efforts on developing interaction with the origins of requirements knowledge. For instance, if it is evident that a partnership with a leading customer provides a source of innovation for the firm, then this partnership should be developed to ensure that a constant stream of ideas is brought into the firm.

3. **The strategic placement of transformation mechanisms** – once transformation mechanisms have been identified, firms should strategically place such mechanisms according to the type and nature of product development projects. For instance, if a particular individual shows exceptional skills in developing business cases in one area of a business, it may be possible to transfer these skills into other business

areas. If a project team completes one project successfully due to the value of the team's collective mix of experience and skills, it may be more prudent to keep the team members together in order to use them on another project.

Consensus and Decision

These two core elements form the sociopolitical aspects of requirements capture. Individuals and groups in organizations mediate the significance attached to requirements knowledge and the origins or requirements knowledge. When deciding upon a product specification, a product development team may be faced with a large amount of possible requirements that may be incorporated into a product concept. Consensus will have to be achieved for the team to continue working in a mutually co-operative fashion. Consensus and a final decision may be achieved democratically, or may occur dictatorially. Bureaucratic and mechanistic methods may take precedence over softer processes.

Requirements Generation

After deciding what the meaning of the gathered information is, this knowledge is used to generate one or more requirements. Taking the example used previously of the customer who preferred red cars, if this data was transformed to mean that the customer was concerned about the image and styling of cars, then the requirement might be generated that the car should look stylish and sporty. As during information transformation, requirements generation is requirements selection. This is too often a tacit process, with certain data being discounted and discarded as irrelevant, most usually because it does not fit with the preconceptions of the individuals or organisation.

Three principles of the generation activity can be identified:

1. **Identification of influencing factors on requirements knowledge** – significant influencing factors need to be identified that may skew the emphasis placed on requirements knowledge and its origin. In business-to-business markets, relationships between competitors and potential customers may need to be taken account of when considering their needs, particularly if customers are playing the market to drive down costs, for instance.
2. **The creation of a level playing field for requirements knowledge** – whatever the nature of requirements knowledge, it needs to come under the fair scrutiny of members of an organization. How this is

achieved is complex, but it may be linked closely to how organizations value their knowledge of the factors that requirements are based on, and the means by which they communicate requirements.

3. **The identification of barriers to consensus and decision making** – factors that may undermine the ability to reach a decision about the creation of a product concept (i.e. the selection of requirements) should be identified. These factors may include financial factors (i.e. the cost of research for instance), requirements knowledge access factors (for instance, some companies may prefer marketing personnel, rather than engineering personnel, to make customer visits), and political factors (top management may need to be included in the decision making).

About this Book

This book is divided into three sections. Section one identifies the key stages in the product development process with respect to the need to innovate – idea generate, design, market launch and evaluate of the product's performance. Whilst the models of this process differ in detail, they agree on the critical events that are needed to create and commercialize new products, regardless of the complexity of the product or the nature of the organization making the product (e.g. service company, small business, etc.).

Section two compares a number of company cases that reveal the processes of RC in different contexts and settings. The cases include technically complex products, such as cars, telecommunications systems, medical textiles, and less technically complex products, but which still demand a high level of expertise, namely a building and a construction tool. For some of the cases, RC is virtually nonexistent and is conducted in a haphazard manner. For others, preproduct planning is a necessity to ensure that stakeholders are involved in the product development process and to prevent silly things happening later on.

Section three presents an RC process that managers in all types of companies can use to help them identify and assess the salient needs that have to be accounted for in the product development process. This process has emerged from working with a number of companies to improve their product development activities to make these streamlined, efficient and cost-effective.

SECTION ONE
Requirements Capture

1   NEW PRODUCT DEVELOPMENT

*Success in innovation appears to depend upon two ingredients –
technical resources (people, equipment, knowledge, money, etc.)
and the capabilities in the organisation to manage them.*

Tidd et al., 1997

The main thrust of requirements capture (RC) occurs at the front end
of product development, but it does not stop there. New requirements
may be discovered during the development of the new product, or
requirements may be modified in the light of user tests. The process
of RC involves collecting, recording and analysing information. The
information gathered will cover markets, customers and technologies. Careful analysis of this leads to the identification of requirements essential for product specification. Integral to the process of
RC is that of identifying the key stakeholders and collecting their
needs, preferences and requirements – and also ensuring that they
buy into the product that is under development. As discussed in the
Introduction, effective RC at the early stages of product development
can contribute positively to quick response, cost and reduce risk.
Companies that invest in the front end of product development are
more likely to produce successful innovations (Cooper and
Kleinschmidt, 1988). However, RC does not stop at the front end of
product development. Effective requirements management is needed
throughout the product development process from inception to commercialization and post-launch. Requirements management is the
activity and process of managing, controlling and refining requirements as the product undergoes development.

In order to establish the relationship between RC and new product development, this chapter highlights the salient aspects of new product development management.

THE NEED FOR PRODUCT DEVELOPMENT

New product development (NPD) is a process that transforms technical ideas or market needs and opportunities into a new product that is launched into the market. Developing new products is an essential aspect of business activity. However, managing the NPD process is complex and risky. It entails managing people who have different backgrounds ranging from marketing to R&D to design. NPD entails substantial investment, both in capital and time. Nonetheless, if it is commercially successful, then the benefits gained are considerable. NPD is a term used to capture a range of different types of innovative activities leading to the production of a new service or product from radical innovations to simple modification and adaptations to existing products. Radical innovation is much more risky and unpredictable. Companies can decide to be first in the market with a radical innovation, or adopt a 'wait and see' approach where they can be followers in a new market. When mobile phones were introduced into the UK market, different technologies were available and the risk for the first mover in the market was related to which technology they should use to operate the mobile service. Hutchinson launched the Rabbit phone using cellular technology and adopted a system of base stations. This failed spectacularly. Within 18 months, and following millions of pounds worth of investment, Rabbit was withdrawn. Competing operators were able to take advantage of the promotional activity associated with mobile phones and attract early adopters of the technology to their service. Backing the wrong technology cost Hutchinson its market advantage and the company was unable to re-enter the market quickly. However, when it did eventually, it launched its Orange service with a vengence and was able to steal a march on its main competitiors.

NEW PRODUCT DEVELOPMENT – THE RELATIONSHIP

Importance of New Product Development

New products enable firms to maintain competitive and healthy product portfolios, and also contribute to long term sustainable competitive advantage. Those companies that fail at NPD may face competitive problems or even collapse (Cooper, 1993). According to Cooper, 'The winners are those firms . . . who have an enviable stream of new product successes year after year'.

A number of factors have a bearing on the importance of NPD, now and for the future. Increased competition in the market place may occur in many ways, e.g. through privatization of government organizations or the increasing power of large multinational companies (Cooper, 1993).

In the increasingly competitive market, the need for time management is essential in order to gain competitive advantage in existing and new markets. A reduced time-to-market is the mechanism for time-based competition (Tersine and Hummingbird, 1995). (See also Cooper 1993; and Coombs 1998.)

> *Speed and Leanness seem increasingly the tombstones of R&D management.*
>
> Coombs, 1988

The product lifecycle (PLC) is based on the belief that most products go through similar sets of stages in their lifetime, from introduction into the market place through to maturity and decline (Bruce, 1997). Product development may occur at any stage of the PLC in order to extend the product's life by rejuvenating the cycle, for example by relaunching the product with new packaging. PLCs are becoming shorter for several reasons, including the increasing sophistication of consumers and improving technology. (See Cooper 1993; and Cooper and Kleinschaft, 1987.)

> *. . . responding to short cycles is a key part of today's hyper-competitive market.*
>
> Grantham, 1997

Emerging foreign markets and globalization can be apparent in a variety of ways, and are vital for NPD in terms of the type of product developed and where the product will be manufactured and sold. For example, the World Trade Organization reached an agreement early in 1997 whereby many developing countries are opening their markets to some degree of competition. Another aspect of emerging foreign markets and globalization is the emergence of low-cost-labour countries becoming more attractive for production from organizations in developing countries (*The Economist*, October 1997). Globalization has many profound effects, not least in the sheer number of markets that have opened up for Western companies. The rapid advances in communication are aiding the rate of globalization through entities such as the Internet and satellite equipment. (See Sheridan, 1998; and Coombs 1998.)

> *Innovation processes are more and more often targeted on global markets . . . Globalisation creates a more demanding innovation process . . .*
>
> Coombs, 1998

The emergence of the European Union (EU) is a major example of a changing business and legislative environment. The EU has enforced the CE mark on certain products manufactured within the EU, which forces manufacturers to comply with certain safety and regulatory standards for the product to be sold in the EU market. (See Wind and Mahajan, 1997.)

The importance of supply chain integration, with factors such as increased competition in all areas, means that companies can no longer rely on their own internal resources and often need to outsource and partner within the supply chain, in order to maintain competitive NPD (Coombs 1998). (See also Sheridan, 1998a.)

Changing customer needs and the rapid pace of technological change affects NPD not only in terms of the product itself, but also in terms of the way the development process is managed and the communication techniques used by the teams involved. For example, globalization of the world market increasingly finds NPD teams in different countries of the world. Virtual project teams that meet via information technology (IT) are increasingly common in that business.

The advantage is that the best talent in the world can be brought together to work on a project. Management of a virtual project team is an emerging management skill. Communication and effectiveness of the teams has improved and contributed to the success of NPD by technologies such as video conferencing. Customers also witness the technological breakthroughs and consequently demand better-quality products faster and at lower prices. (see Cooper, 1993; and Coombs, 1998.)

Strategic Management of Product Development

The management of NPD must be considered in a strategic fashion, in order that the right type of product may be developed in terms of, for example, the target market, the company resources, and the company product portfolio. A nonstrategic approach to NPD may involve development of a highly technological product, but if the market does not have a need for this type of product, it will fail, even though it may be a superior product. Marketing and promotion and identifying the channels to reach the customer are all essential to the innovation process. Tidd et al. (1997) define a number of advantages that can be gained through strategic NPD projects (Table 1.1). This table accentuates the importance of strategy in NPD. Although a certain type of new product may offer a strategic advantage, the organization must assess how the product strategy fits into the overall strategy of the organization.

Table 1.1   Type of innovation by strategic advantage

Type of innovation	Strategic advantage
Novelty	Offering something, that no-one else can
Competence shifting	Rewriting the rules of the competence game
Complexity	Difficulty of learning about technology keeps entry barriers high
Robust design	Basic model product or process can be stretched over an extended life, reducing overall cost
Continuous incremental innovation	Continuous movement of cost–performance frontier

Source: Tidd et al., 1997. Reprinted by permission of John Wiley and Sons Ltd.

Some academics and writers suggest that NPD is not the important strategy for future success of organizations, but rather that sustained competitive advantage is to be gained through intelligent marketing, as mentioned in Bissell (1998). However, new products not only account for 40 per cent of total company sales, but they are also important for profits and market share (Cooper, 1993). Deloitte and Touche (1980) conducted a study, *1998 Vision in Manufacturing*, which showed that by 2000, a majority of manufacturing companies plan to intensify and re-engineer their NPD efforts. It is estimated that over this time, revenues from the sale of new products will have increased by 11 per cent (Sheridan, 1998b).

Cost or Investment?

Companies regard NPD as a costly process. The failure rates of new products are extremely high and have not improved much since NPD was first studied (Wind and Mahajan, 1997) so the cost in relation to failure rate is an important issue. Tidd et al. (1997) suggest failure rates of new products to be between 30 and 95 per cent, with an accepted average of 38 per cent. In addition to this, Cooper (1993) states that 46 per cent of total product costs spent on NPD are used entirely on products that fail and that one in three new products fail at launch. This issue of failure in NPD highlights the enormous importance of achieving effective management of NPD, to reduce the failure rate of new products. This emphasises the need for RC to tighten up the front end of the product development process to improve the success rate.

Success in New Product Development

Much has been written on what contributes to success in NPD. There are a number of factors that contribute to the success of a new product, although it is unlikely that any organization would be able to institute a formula for persistent success in NPD (Wind and Mahajan, 1997).

Cooper (1993) has carried out several extensive studies on the success in NPD. He divides success factors into three categories: luck, tailwind and actions. In his study *NewProd III*, he studied 203 new product projects in 125 industrial product firms. All the new products were launched on to the market – some were successful, some failed. The study compared the similarities in successes and the differences between winners and losers. Several significant factors emerged, resulting in ten key factors underlying success:

1. A superior product that delivers unique benefits to the user.
2. A well-defined product prior to the development phase.
3. Quality of execution of technical activities.
4. Technological synergy.
5. Quality of execution of predevelopment activities.
6. Market synergy.
7. Quality of execution of marketing activities.
8. Market attractiveness.
9. Competitive situation.
10. Top management support.

Of the hundreds of characteristics studied, only these ten had consistent impact on success, although not all had the same impact. The results of the study showed that luck could be ruled out as a success factor, and that tailwind and actions were the important factors in successful NPD, with action factors being of particular importance.

Hart (1995) has developed six major themes for success in NPD, which can be considered at project level or strategic level (Figure 1.1).

Project Level Themes

Process

> The process of NPD involves that activities and decisions from the time when an idea is generated (from whatever source) until the product is commercialised (i.e., launched onto the market).
>
> Hart, 1995

Many studies, for example Cooper (1979, 1980), and Cooper and Kleinschmidt (1987), state that the choice of process for NPD is vital to the success of the project (Hart, 1995). An important consideration when choosing a process is the contingent circumstances that apply to the particular process (Tidd et al., 1997) (see Table 1.2).

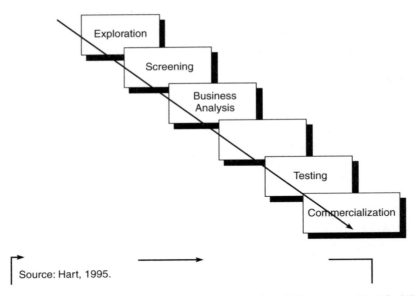

Source: Hart, 1995.

Figure 1.1   The process of NPD as a series of activities, from Hart S. (1995) in Bruce and Biemans. Reprinted by permission of John Wiley and Sons.

Table 1.2   How context affects NPD process

Context variable	Modifiers to the basic process
Sector	Different sectors have different priorities and characteristics, e.g. scale-intensive or science-intensive
Size	Small firms differ in terms of access to resources, etc. and so need to develop more linkages
National systems of innovation	Different countries have more or less supportive contexts in terms of institutions, policies, etc.
Lifecycle (of technology, industry, etc.)	Different stages in lifecycle emphasise different aspects of innovation, e.g. new technology industries versus mature, established firms

Source: Tidd et al., 1997. Reprinted by permission of John Wiley and Sons Ltd.

Early Sequential Models of New Product Development

Linear models were developed in recognition of the fact that each stage of the process has to be completed, in order that the product should have more chance of being successful (Cooper and Kleinschmidt, 1986). However, these sequential models are regarded as relatively simple, standard processes for NPD.

The Booz, Allen and Hamilton (1982) model (Figure 1.1) shows the basic sequential approach to the NPD process. This model is the basis for a large number of similar sequential type models, including those of Kotler (1980) and the British Standards Institute (1989)

Cooper and Kleinschmidt (1986) focused more closely on the process of NPD. They produced a 13-stage model with distinct activities at each stage (Table 1.3). Crawford (1988) simplified the Cooper and Kleinschmidt model into six stages (Table 1.4).

However, these sequential models tend to be prescriptive and mechanistic, and fail to take into account overlaps of activities that will occur naturally in the workplace. They can also increase cycle time and provide no early warning system for problems that may occur later in the process (Schilling and Hill, 1998). The weaknesses apparent in the sequential models led to the development of more complex models.

Later Complex Models of New Product Development

> *Concurrent engineering has become the norm for successful product development.*
>
> Design News, 1993

Increased competition in the market place has placed more pressure on companies involved in NPD to reduce their time to market or to gain quick response. Products have become more complicated resulting in more people being involved from a variety of functions (Jones, 1997). This has brought about the more complex parallel processing in NPD models, which reduce time to market, provide smoother transition between stages of the process, promote shared responsibility, co-operation, involvement and commitment, and improve the problem-solving focus, initiative, diversified skills and heightened sensitivity to market conditions (Hart, 1995).

Table 1.3   Cooper and Kleinschmidt's 13-stage model of the NPD process

Activity	Description
1. Initial screening	The initial go/no go decision where it was first decided to allocate the funds to the proposed new product idea
2. Preliminary market assessment	An initial, preliminary, but nonscientific market assessment; a first quick look at the market
3. Preliminary technical assessment	An initial, preliminary appraisal of the technical merits and difficulties of the project
4. Detailed market study/market research	Marketing research, involving a reasonable sample of respondents, a formal design and a consistent data collection procedure
5. Business/financial analysis	A financial or business analysis leading to a go/no go decision prior to product development
6. Product development	The actual design and development of the product, resulting in, for example, a prototype or sample product
7. In-house product testing	Testing the product in house, in the lab or under controlled conditions
8. Customer tests of product	Testing the products under real-life conditions, e.g. with customers and/or in the field
9. Test market/trial sell	A test market or trial sell of the product – trying to sell
10. Trial production	A trial production run to test the production facilities
11. Precommercialization business analysis	A financial or business analysis, following product development but prior to full-scale launch
12. Production start-up	The start-up of full-scale or commercial production
13. Market launch	The launch of the product, on a full-scale and/or commercial basis; an identifiable set of marketing activities specific to this product

Source: Hart, 1995.

Table 1.4 Crawford's six-stage model of the NPD process

Activity	Description
1. New product planning	Emphasising NPD as an element of corporate planning process
2. Idea generation	Seeking ideas internally and externally (from management, research, competition, consumers and employees)
3. Screening	To analyse corporate and technical synergy and feasibility of the project
4. Technical development	Concepts developed into physical forms
5. Market appraisal	To assess user opinions
6. Commercialization	Launch of the product or service

Source: Roberts, 1996

Sequential models provide a good basis for planning projects, but in practice, the process is often comprised of '... a parallel set of sub-activities in which the technical and marketing disciplines interact to evaluate and develop further the product concept' (Walsh et al., 1992). These parallel processing models involve overlapping stages in the NPD process (Hart, 1995). Takeuchi and Nonaka (1986) produced a diagram showing the differences between the sequential and complex models of NPD (Figure 1.2).

Walsh et al. (1992) show in a fairly simple fashion a number of different approaches to the NPD process corresponding to the Takeuchi and Nonaka (1986) diagram. This approach is designed in an attempt to break down the functional barriers between departments, so that activities in the NPD process are carried out concurrently. The process is therefore managed by multidisciplinary teams, meaning that the outcome is owned by all functions. Thus ideas are not rejected by downstream partners as they may be in the sequential processes. Information is shared by functions, which allows functions time to prepare and position themselves for future stages of the project. This approach reduces the time to market, avoids bottlenecks and improves quality.

The major benefit of concurrent engineering in NPD is that it speeds up time to market by reducing the cycle time (Anderson, 1993 and Biemans, 1995). In addition, the needs of the project are better

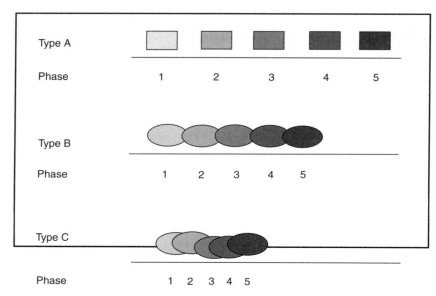

Figure 1.2   Sequential (A) versus overlapping (B and C) phases of development, from The New Product Development Game by Hirotaka Takeuchi and Ikujiro Nonaka (1986), Harvard Business Review.

satisfied (Jones, 1997). There are some limitations to parallel processing. Generally, these types of projects require more effort from all concerned, and more effective management. Some types of product development projects are not suitable for parallel processing, for example, R&D-led projects require a large amount of time at the beginning stages and cannot be integrated easily (Jones, 1997).

Parallel processing requires large-scale organizational changes in the entire supply chain, and many companies may be unwilling to introduce this during recession (Palframan, 1994). In reality, most companies are not willing to deal with the culture shock that accompanies a change in routine. Most organizations tend to provide quick one-shot programmes that do not do much to alter the traditional method of NPD (Anderson, 1993).

In the concurrent NPD process, it is critical that the traditionally separate functions of design and manufacturing are merged. However, in practice, combining the two can be difficult in terms of logistics and in relation to issues of diversity (Anderson, 1993).

Table 1.5   The results of phase review

Result	Implication
Pass – all deliverables complete and objectives met	Move on to next phase
Conditional pass – minor actions identified	Project can move on to next phase if actions are completed to the satisfaction of the chairperson within 30 days
Fail first time – major problems identified	Review will recommend to business that further investment be withheld
Conditional fail – major problems identified	Major corrective action required; rerun review within 30 days having cleared actions
Fail second time	Review with business about whether project should be cancelled

Source: Grammer, 1992

Communication between functions is also essential, for example in terms of sharing information. However, geographic location can be a hindrance to this, so electronic communication is becoming increasingly important. For example, members of the design group at AT&T in the USA work in the parallel process, communicating between the manufacturing site in Denver and the design labs, which are 1500 miles away in New Jersey, by fax, email, teleconferencing and high-speed data links.

> *...the two areas have been able to achieve their goal, which was to improve circuit-pack design and manufacturability.*
>
> Anderson, 1993

RC falls into the front-end and early phases of these models. Requirements management is needed throughout the product development process to ensure that all relevant information is gathered from key stakeholders in the process (e.g. marketing, technology, design) and that this is used to optimize the requirements that will enhance the attractiveness of the product for its target market.

Alternative Approaches to New Product Development Process

The Phase Review Process – First Generation

The first-generation model of this process was based on the sequential process of NPD, similar in features to a relay race, and was developed by NASA in 1960. Each activity has a review point (Grammer, 1992), which evaluates certain criteria, such as:

- performance
- reliability
- availability
- instability
- maintainability
- usability
- testability
- manufacturability
- profitability
- timeliness

This is to decide whether or not more funding should be allocated, and whether the project should continue. According to Grammer (1992), the phase review process helps the organization to:

- *Authorise* any project in terms of return on investment and risk analysis before major resources are committed.
- *Apply* the disciplines and project management that enable businesses to bring a product to market against challenging time and cost targets.
- *Define* customer requirements and expectations clearly and prove that these have been met prior to delivery.
- *Ensure* that product announcements and availability dates are consistent with achieving key milestones.

Cooper (1994) analysed the first-generation phase review process and emphasised several problems associated with the model. In general, the main problem was the number of tasks that had to be completed at each stage before the project could progress. The process was too narrowly focused, ignoring all stages except development and failing to integrate marketing functions in the process.

Table 1.6   The advantages and disadvantages of the stage gate process over the phase review process

Advantages	Disadvantages
Better cross-functional teamwork	Projects must wait until all tasks are completed; this may lead to delays, as a project may be held for the sake of one activity that remains to be completed
Less reworking and recycling	Overlapping of stages is impossible; one stage has to be completed before a project can move on to another
The early detention of failures	Projects must go through all stages and gates; this can make the process very rigid, especially for low-risk projects, and may create unnecessary delay
A better launch	Project prioritization is not accounted for as the stage gate concentrates on individual projects rather than the spectrum of product portfolio projects
A shorter time to market	Some processes are spelt out in too much detail, leaving no room for creativity
Not a rigid system – some stages may be omitted	Too bureaucratic because of the imposed meeting, paperwork and red tape

Third-Generation Models

Cooper (1994) agrees that the stage gate models provided improvement in process, but require improvements to allow better integration and flexibility. He therefore developed the third-generation models, which he described as '. . . fluid and adaptable, they will incorporate fuzzy gates which are both situational and conditional, they will provide for much sharper focus of resources and management of the portfolio of projects, and they will be much more flexible than today's process'.

Table 1.7 The four types of partnerships

Supplier partnerships	Lateral partnerships	Internal partnerships	Buyer partnerships
Goods suppliers	Competitors	Business units	Intermediate customers
Services suppliers	Non-profit organizations	Employees Functional departments	Ultimate customers

A fluid process should reduce the cycle time because stages will be overlapped. The notion of 'fuzzy gates' implies that the gates are not absolute, but are considered more in terms of the 'situational' and 'conditional' factors involved. The clearer focus is achieved, as the third-generation models are compared against other projects. The process is, in essence, a formal process with rules and protocol. A deviation from these rules should be carried out consciously and deliberately with awareness of the consequences. However, project managers should be given the freedom to make these decisions, because of their greater experience with the project, and management should back the decision (Cooper, 1994).

The stage gate system is used to improve efficiency and effectiveness of the NPD process. The gates are used to control the process and provide a quality control checkpoint. Each stage is used to gather information to progress to the next stage in order to drive down uncertainties. The stage gate system is designed to facilitate and speed up time to market (Cooper, 1993). Stage gate systems incorporate many of the factors for success in NPD and reinforce the role of RC, for example:

- More emphasis on predevelopment activities (discussed in Chapter 3).
- Multidisciplinary and multifunctional.
- Parallel processing speeds up process.
- Strong market orientation is part of the stage gate system.
- More focus.
- Product definition step is included.
- Focus on quality of execution.

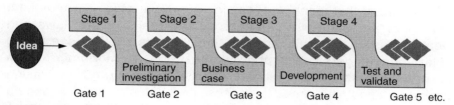

Figure 1.3 Third generation process with overlapping, fluid stages, and 'fuzzy' or conditional go decisions
Source: Roberts, 1996

> *The benefits of the stage gate system are evident. The model puts discipline into a process, that in too many firms, is ad hoc and seriously deficient.*
>
> Cooper, 1993

The Stage Gate Decision

Evaluation techniques, such as stage gates, are used in order to reduce uncertainty and make go/no go decisions in NPD. Evaluation is different at each gate and deals with a variety of different complexities (Cooper, 1993), including:

- The information and stakes at each gate increases through the process.
- There are a variety of methods of evaluation to use at each stage, requiring a decision for the best technique to be used for each gate.
- At each gate the decision on the go/no go basis has to be made in relation to the portfolio of products that the company is developing. There will always be certain payoffs to other projects.
- The go/no go decision actually involves a go/no go/hold/recycle decision.

So the purposes of the gate, according to Cooper (1993), are:

- To make go/no go decisions.
- To make prioritization decisions.
- To serve as a quality control check.
- To chart the path forward.

It is important that managers look for 'killer' variables, for too often, managers proceed with a project without realising the flaws and weaknesses, leading ultimately to failure. This may be due to the failure of managers to accept problems or to seek more information on problems when they become apparent (Cooper, 1993). Making decisions about the product, its cost and potential market benefit are all relevant to requirements management. RC fits in with a stage gate process.

According to Cooper, any project can be reduced to three simple questions:

- Is it real?
- Is it worth it?
- Can we win?

Cooper describes a typical approach to a project team stage gate decision. Stage gate decisions are usually based on written criteria (it should be noted that too much bureaucracy can delay projects and reduce time to market). The project leader will submit a set of deliverables/inputs a few days before the meeting. These should be short and to the point, e.g. some organizations may place a limit on the number of sides used to write this. Gatekeepers receive copies to prepare for the meeting. At the meeting, the project leader will bring any new team members up to date, although in many organizations, the gatekeepers are the same throughout the project. A question-and-answer session is used to share information and opinions. Gatekeepers use evaluation techniques to decide the go/no go decision, with each criterion being discussed.

Debriefing is important so that the gatekeepers can reflect on the opinions of others in the project team, and thus perhaps operate more efficiently as a team for other projects. This may include (Cooper 1993):

- areas of disagreement;
- areas of ignorance and uncertainty;
- strengths and weaknesses of the project;
- go/no go decision reached; and
- prioritization set.

Despite the support for the stage gate process in much of the literature, there are some schools of thought that suggest that the stage
gate system is not as successful as described. Although it is designed
to work in a parallel process, it often becomes a linear process. Wind
and Mahajan (1997) depict the stage gate process as shown in Figure
1.4. They describe the gate process as 'cumbersome and inappropriate'. Nevertheless, RC is an important aspect of the process and
needs to be seen with the process description and activity.

Communication

RC and requirements management is dependent on effective communication between key activities, especially marketing, production,
finance and design. Without empathy for each other and an understanding of each other's needs, then agreement about the main
requirements to build into the product will be difficult to achieve.
Engineering may argue for a greater performance or range of functions than marketing regard as necessary for the target market, and

Figure 1.4 Wind and Mahajan's diagram of the stage gate process.
Reprinted with permission from *Journal of Marketing Research*, published
by the American Marketing Association, Wind, J. and Mahajan, V., 1997, Vol.
XXXIV and p. 1–12

so on. Cross-functional project teams can speed up communication between departments such as marketing, R&D and manufacturing, all of which are vital for the NPD process (Schilling and Hill, 1998; and Calabrese, 1997).

Functional integration can reduce time to market, save costs, and improve communication so that any potential problems can be detected early on in the process (Hart, 1995). Cross-functional teams should also minimize mis-communication, provide a broader knowledge base, increase the cross-fertilization of ideas, draw from more information sources and increase the fit between product attributes and customer requirements (Schilling and Hill, 1998). In addition to these advantages, functional integration ensures alignment of product concept with company and functional strategy and promotes concurrent engineering (Verganti, 1997). Tidd et al. (1997) describe the problems that can results if full integration does not occur. One of the most consistent problems in multifunctional teams is the failure to include those from outside the loop.

The extent of integration of the R&D and marketing functions has traditionally been the focus of research, due to the importance of their integration for the success of the NPD process (Hart, 1995).

> *The R&D/marketing interface is critical for new product success.*
> Wang, 1997

These two areas are traditionally uncooperative – there is often a debate as to which department should drive the NPD process. The R&D and marketing functions tend to grow and become increasingly specialized in their own field as the organization grows larger (Wang, 1997). Close collaboration between R&D and marketing enables the production of a product that fits well with customer requirements. R&D cannot design a product that fits with customer requirements without contribution from marketing (Schilling and Hill, 1998). Wang (1997) defines four kinds of barrier to good interface between R&D and marketing.

1. *Perpetual* – a study by Gupta et al. in 1986 proved that the personality traits of R&D and marketing managers were similar,

thus the barrier between the two is actually more of perceived stereotypes rather than actual differences.

2. *Cultural* – resulting from training in different backgrounds.
3. *Organizational* – arising from different task priorities, ambiguity, tolerance and departmental structures.
4. *Language* – marketing managers and R&D managers have different terminology that is specific to their training and area of expertise, making communication between the two very difficult.

Techniques are available to those involved in NPD to encourage communication between these two functions. For example, quality function deployment (QFD) is designed for engineering production and marketing functions to identify opportunities for product improvements or differentiation. Customer requirement characteristics can be translated through a matrix so that the engineers can understand them (Tidd et al., 1997). However, integration may be simpler than employing tools such as these. Promoting teamwork through exercises, and teaching team and team leader skills and related communicative skills (Anderson, 1993), can promote company-wide skills that can be exploited in the NPD process.

Souder (1988) describes the ways in which organizations should attempt to integrate the R&D and marketing functions:

- Make personnel aware that interface problems occur naturally.
- Make personnel sensitive to the characteristics of disharmony.
- Give equal praise to both functions.
- Continuously reinforce their desire for R&D and marketing collaboration.
- Use teams of R&D and marketing personnel at every opportunity.
- Solve personality clashes as soon as possible.
- Avoid complacency – too much harmony is a bad thing.

Although the benefits and advantages of functional integration have been outlined, it should be noted that there are a few problems with function integration. Firstly, the depth of knowledge within each function has decreased because individuals are spending too much time on product development projects, rather than their own function. Involvement in both NPD projects and functional activities can also result in individuals feeling torn between the respective managers of each area (Sobek et al., 1998). Finally, it is often impossible in today's business environment to actually get all the project team together for every meeting. The global feature of many organizations today means that certain functions of the firm may be in a different country or, at the very least, several hundred miles away. Many project teams function on the basis that the whole team has to be present at every meeting, but it is possible to achieve resourceful input from team members in different ways, e.g. through electronic or telecommunication or through partial collocation.

THE ENTIRE SUPPLY CHAIN INTEGRATION

Most industry sectors are becoming more competitive, with customers making higher demands upon suppliers and products. Inevitably, in response to these constraints, new management philosophies are introduced. One such philosophy to be applied is supply chain integration and partnering. There has always been a plethora of collaborative strategies, such as co-makership, co-design relationships, strategic alliance, network, hybrid organization, virtual organization, concurrent engineering, and parallel product development, which facilitate co-development.

Formal partnerships vary from full joint alliances to collaborative R&D. Relationship management theory proposes four types of partnerships (Table 1.7). Whether the relationships are formal or informal, didactic or multiple, the information and knowledge held throughout the entire supply chain is extremely beneficial to the innovation and product development process.

Partnerships are considered as a means of harnessing more effectively the knowledge and skills in the supply chain in order to compete in a global market place. A three-stage strategic development programme is proposed by DTI (1995) consisting of survival, bootstrapping and expansion. The survival stage is based on the prerequisite that the company must keep hold of its present position by meeting customer basic needs. Bootstrapping involves gaining knowledge and experience from customers and partners and utilizing this to improve internal performance. The expansion stage represents the application of new skills into product development and geographic markets. All stages demand the development of expertise in accessing information and data for new product development; establishing a good RC process that enables the capture of information throughout the entire supply chain from third- and fourth-tier suppliers through to end users is vitally important. However a more integrated and better-managed supplier, through relationship management and partnering, will facilitate easier and more accurate RC.

CONCLUSION

Product development and innovation management are necessary aspects of business. Despite all our knowledge about process management, the concurrent engineering, and effective interface between key activities, a high failure rate exists. What has been ignored is a detailed review of the early stages of the process. It is here that the need for a new product, or modifications, is decided and ideas generated for consideration. Once the idea has been selected for development, then it is difficult to abort the project because of the investments that have been made in this idea. If more attention were given to the front end of the process, in terms of creativity management and ascertaining the key product requirements, and subsequently to requirements management, then the outcome may be more successful.

2

REQUIREMENTS: IDEAS, RESEARCH AND STRATEGY

...the greatest differences between winners and losers were found in the quality of execution of predevelopment activities...we saw little widespread evidence of firms using anything that resembled a formal new product process or new product game plan: indeed the typical process was random, chaotic and in too many cases out of control.

Cooper and Kleinschmidt (1993)

Product development is about creating products for the future. Customer needs are constantly changing and so companies have to address the needs of future customers as well as those of their current ones. New technologies are another driving force in innovation and these need to be harnessed to meet new needs and to create products. Product development occurs in a dynamic context and is future-oriented. Consequently, it is about risk and entrepreneurship. At the start of a new project, the outcome of this cannot be certain. Firms have to choose between a number of potentially lucrative ideas. The dilemma is the risk of rejecting the right idea or accepting the wrong one in the early phase. The levels of uncertainty are caused by a number of factors in the early stages of NPD, including:

- dynamic environments (both internal and external);
- incomplete information;
- ambiguous situations;
- poor clarity of objectives;
- time pressure leading to lack of reflection and a focus on progression;

- intense political activity within firm;
- strong reliance on tacit knowledge, gut feel and intuition;
- subjectivism and bias; and
- high degree of behavioural changes (individual, group and organizational).

Management practice for capturing requirements at the fuzzy front end of NPD is limited. Notions of what constitutes the early stages of NPD are wide ranging (Urban and Hauser, 1980 and Wind, 1982), and so the creative aspects of RC never cease during NPD. Companies have to be alert to new discoveries and changes in market opportunities that can affect their ideas for new products. Bailetti and Guild (1991) suggest that companies lack the ability to generate operational definitions of new opportunities. In another study, Feldman and Page (1984) found 'no real attempt at formal management of the idea flow and there was little evidence of formality in the idea screening procedures.' Cooper and Kleinschidt (1993) describe this process as 'random, chaotic and in too many cases out of control.' Good reasons exist for this state of affairs. Firstly, a 'rational' approach may not be appropriate. Secondly, intuition and having a gut feel for the potential of an idea is part of RC and this relies on key individuals thinking abstractly about the potential of an idea in terms of the market, technology and the likely impact of company resources. But whatever the source of the good idea, it is the management of this process that is the key to ensuring that the right product is selected for development. Dealing with RC can be reduced to three key questions:

- How do concepts for new products come about?
- What information is required to define an idea?
- How does one assess the potential of these ideas in the first instance?

RC depends upon knowledge, research and ideas. It is a highly creative activity and requires managers to recognize the potential of the knowledge they possess to become translated into new product requirements. In other words, knowledge has to be acquired and then transformed into ideas that form the basis of product requirements. This chapter focuses on three core activities of RC: idea generation; research; and strategy. Knowledge flows and organizational learning are discussed principally, as these relate to RC. This chapter also considers how the knowledge used to create new products and services is acquired, what organizational structures impinge on this, and how individuals and groups within organizations behave in the early phases of NPD.

THE CLASSICAL VIEW OF THE EARLY STAGES OF NEW PRODUCT DEVELOPMENT

Classical approaches to management of the front end of NPD imply that a formal process can be imposed to manage the complex and uncertain environment (e.g. Cooper and Kleinschmidt, 1993, Piercy (1989) describes formal product development processes as 'characterized by the existence of discrete decision areas, defined by formalized frameworks, using information collected and analysed through a set of accepted scientific techniques.'

This classical view describes the early stages of NPD as a place where strategic product/market decisions are made in the light of corporate strategy and where the concepts for products and services emerge in their raw state. This view is particularly in favour of formalization of business processes in response to a complex and uncertain environment.

Common to these models is an emphasis on single projects as units of product development. This ignores the fact that there may be several projects underway simultaneously, which, when viewed holistically, are developing a firm's overall product development knowledge base. In addition, such concurrent project environments can trigger the cross-fertilization of ideas.

These projects may well exert unpredictable demands on a firm's resources. Thus a change in the path of one project may affect the outcome of another and result in opportunity costs. This is particularly acute when firms have to choose between, and prioritize, a number of potentially lucrative product ideas (Whelan, 1988).

The dilemma that firms face is the risk of rejecting the right idea or accepting the wrong one in the early stages of NPD. Whilst spending time and money on idea generation and definition is important to ascertain the nature of the risk for each idea, and the potential of every idea may not be sufficiently understood, firms may be confronted with a large number of ideas.

Ideas must be defined before they can be appraised and assessed. In the early stages, idea assessment and definition are closely related and will rely on key individuals thinking abstractly about the potential of an idea in terms of the market, competitors and its likely impact on company resources. Such individuals tend to rely on their firm's knowledge base. Depending on whether resources permit, and according to the level of detail required, these individuals may

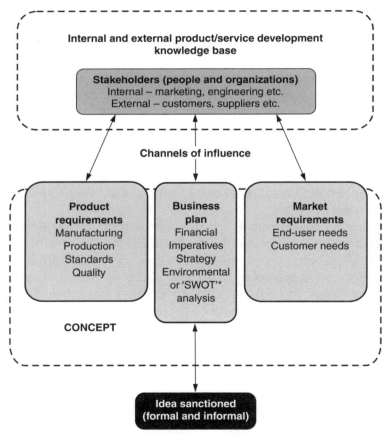

* Strengths, Weaknesses, Opportunities and Threats

Figure 2.1 Defining and assessing ideas

carry out various activities to gain a clearer picture of the product or service concept, such as informal discussions and focused research activities using out-of-house market research agencies.

Information that assists in the definition and assessment can be gathered, ranging from product requirements, market requirements and financial requirements (Figure 2.1). As this figure suggests, individuals tap into the internal and external knowledge base to define and assess product and service ideas. Those with the responsibility for defining and assessing ideas will act as a conduit for other 'stakeholders' preferences, opinions and knowledge, and social and political bias, and this will affect the process. For instance large customers may well have greater influence in shaping the mix of requirements than other stakeholders. (Stakeholders are defined as individuals or groups of individuals whose preferences, opinions and knowledge are perceived to be significant by an organization engaged in generating, defining and assessing ideas for products and services.)

SOFT PROCESSES

In recent years, such classical approaches as described above have been questioned. McDonough and Leifer (1986) submit that 'unfortunately, in new product development projects ... tasks are ambiguous and unfamiliar, innovation can not be programmed in advance.' Rickards (1991) advises that 'linear models of the innovation process have been consistently wanting both in practical and in theoretical examinations of the subject, and concludes that current models do not reflect the creative and innovative behaviour of individuals and organizations. Rothwell (1992), Bosomworth and Sage (1995) and Pavia (1991) highlight the importance of informal processes versus formal processes, particularly in the early stages of new product development.

These soft processes include serendipity (for example, the natural cross-fertilization of ideas), intuition, experience, intrapreneurship and entrepreneurship, organizational and individual learning and creativity, politics, power and relationships (personal, interfunctional and interfirm). These are not accounted for formally in the classical models.

Core Early Stage Activities

This chapter proposes that these soft factors are critical to facilitating the emergence of ideas in organizations. In effect, such factors represent the coupling of technical ideas with market opportunities referred to by Freeman (1982), Tidd (1993) and Faulkner (1994). Tidd describes the early stages as where 'market opportunities, technological opportunities and economic feasibility are translated into a new product concept.' Similarly, Faulkner suggests that 'success in industrial innovation rests on the effective organizational coupling of technical and market opportunities.'

Rather than looking at stages or steps of a particular product development project, activities that occur at the front end, i.e. the activities that lead up to the emergence of a concept for a product or service, are identified. From the literature, three major activities are associated with innovative behaviour at the early stages of product development, namely idea generation, research and strategy-centred activities. These activities are illustrated in Figure 2.2. They are not restricted to functional remits. Marketing, production and design personnel, can take part, initiate or intervene, to some degree, in NPD activities.

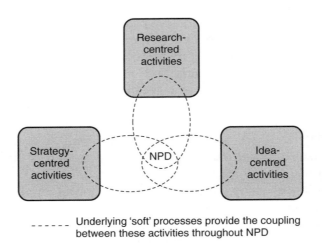

‑ ‑ ‑ ‑ ‑ ‑ Underlying 'soft' processes provide the coupling
between these activities throughout NPD

Figure 2.2 Model of research, strategy- and idea-centred activities for NPD

Much of the NPD literature presumes that idea generation, research and strategy-centred activities are restricted mainly to the front end of the process. Yet individuals and groups interpret and process information at whatever stage in the development process they find themselves using a variety of sources, not just scientific research activities. Thus, depending on how broadly or narrowly one defines research, research-centred activities may happen at any time in product development, or may even occur outside it, and have little to do with the product development project at hand. Similarly, idea-centred activities are located predominately in the predevelopment activities of the product development process (Cooper, 1988), yet many new ideas for products and services may surface further downstream in the development process or come from external sources, out of the control of the organization. The very existence of innovation schemes in large multinational companies, such as 3M (Ranganath and Ketteringham 1987), gives credence to the fact that ideas can emerge from any part of an organization, or from outside it, at any point in time. This means that RC management is an activity that is fundamental to innovation management. If RC is documented once the project commences, and is linked clearly with strategic objectives, then changes can be related back to the original objectives and modifications made accordingly. Without this reference point, changes can be made in an ad hoc manner and affect the success of the project.

The view that strategy is 'frozen' at the start of product development in the form of a corporate plan (encompassing marketing, technology and financial imperatives) is also losing credence, as is the idea that the very existence of an explicit strategy is an important factor for innovation. For instance Inkpen (1995) argues that constructive ambiguity (the absence of strategy) can be linked to innovative improvements. An obvious tension exists between a firm's plan for the future based on imperfect information and uncertainty and the realization that until those plans are implemented then the future will remain transient and indeterminable. Strategy is an ongoing emergent process, allowing for contingencies, flexibility and a firm's adaptive learning behaviour in the face of a complex and dynamic competitive environment (Mintzberg and Quinn 1991; Meyers, 1990).

Idea-Centred Activities

Researchers have defined the front end of the product innovation process as concept generation (Cramp, 1994), exploration (Booz et al., 1982), opportunity identification (Urban and Hauser, 1980), idea generation (Wind, 1982), a search process (Conway and McGuinness, 1986), and idea development (Myers and Marquis, 1969). Viewing the front end as a process by which companies find the right ideas to develop has led many researchers to try to link idea types. In this kind of research, it is evident that various methodological problems exist concerning what constitutes an idea (i.e. is it a mental construct, a belief, a market opportunity, a product prototype, a design visual, a design specification, or a shared meaning or understanding?). Ideas can be generated in collaboration with suppliers or other parties involved in collaborative NPD.

Ideas can come from both internal and external sources. There is much discussion in the literature concerning which area is the most productive, both in terms of the number of ideas produced and the impact the source of ideas has on new product performance (Cooper, 1981; and Cooper and Kleinschmidt, 1993). Myers and Marquis (1969) found that '62% of the innovations arose from internal channels, such as personal contacts, experimentation, and R&D, and 32% from external channels, such as contact with the vendor, experiences outside the firm and research papers.' Conway and McGuinness (1986) state that ideas can be sought from:

- strategy, goals and organizational memory;
- preferences and 'pet' ideas of individuals;
- information on market developments;
- information on technical developments;
- customer problems; and
- trigger events (such as a fundamental change in technology, standards, regulation etc.).

Other variables have also been suggested as affecting idea generation (Rochford, 1991):

Planning efficient discussion, hard agreements on meeting frequently and duration, diversity in participant backgrounds, multiple inputs, training and experience of the idea generators, organizational and managerial commitment, allocation of priority to new project development, personal motivation, the firm's reward system, and the firm's ability to absorb related risk of failure are suggested as factors which can affect idea generation success.

By contrast, techniques are methods that can be employed to generate new product ideas, such as brainstorming. Screening procedures are presented in the literature as objective criteria-based methods, of choosing between ideas (see Figure 2.3). Thus, broadly speaking, a member of a company can choose to visit a customer (source) and have a discussion (technique) in order to find, trigger, detect, explore, discover, collect, generate, invent and/or search for product ideas (Root-Bernstein, 1989).

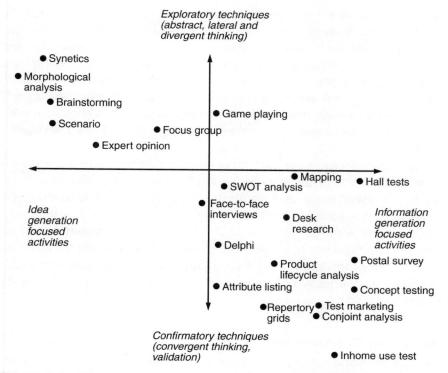

Figure 2.3 Techniques for generating information, knowledge and ideas

Yet such techniques may deny the benefits of random scanning (which has no deliberate purpose) where serendipity comes to the fore. However, if random scanning were to be defined, it may also become an accepted technique. Using a particular technique may well effect directly the nature of ideas that emerge. For instance, firms who want to explore and generate 'blue sky' ideas may well employ a different set of idea generation techniques to a firm that is focused on incremental development of products. Chapter 3 examines the different market research tools and techniques by market research specialists at the front end of NPD.

Firms may have ideas that are not in a commercially accessible form. Thus the firm is uncertain of their value and research activities are undertaken to gain a better understanding of their value.

Creative Leadership

To generate ideas, the company needs an environment conducive to creativity and a team that works well together. Rickards and Moger (1999) suggest that there are three types of creative team. Dream Teams, Standard Teams and Teams from Hell. Dream Teams are likely to have more successful ideas than the other two. Rickards and Moger suggest that seven factors can be used to assess a team's performance. These are: platform of understanding; vision; climate; ideas; response to setbacks; network skills; and, response to experience.

In addition, creative leadership is essential to facilitate the creative team. In their experience, creative leaders seek win–win situations, are highly motivating use strategies and techniques to encourage team members to solve problems, and have the ability to align individual needs with team goals. Du Pont is a company that excels at creative management. Personnel at all levels are encouraged to avoid factors that might inhibit creativity and to experiment with different ideas without regard to current knowledge, experience or expertise.

Identifying Opportunities

The role of individuals and groups as members of a social and political milieu are particularly important when one looks at the process of how ideas in organizations are sanctioned both formally and informally (Van de Ven and Walker 1984; and Van de Ven, 1986). For instance, the literature suggests that once a number of ideas emerge, these are then filtered; screened or evaluated in order to find the best opportunities (Sowrey, 1989; Bosomworth and Sage 1995). This literature infers that an objective formal group activity takes place. By contrast, other researchers have found that the identification of an opportunity worth pursuing was initially often based on the judgment of one or a few key individuals (Conway and McGuinness, 1986). Such key individuals may be the only ones who really have an adequate, in-depth understanding of applying certain criteria, such as 'fit with strategy', and will need to be steeped in the organization's practices and traditions as a result. Thus as Rochford (1991) suggests, in terms of idea evaluation criteria in the first instance, 'management opinion may be the only "data" available.' In this sense, criteria-based methods rely on agreed measures usually formed through consensus of key individuals at a strategic level (Brownlie and Spender, 1995). Such measures are therefore highly tacit, value-laden and subject to social and political influences.

Thus, a further tension in objective screening processes is that key individuals may well have formulated the screening criteria themselves and taken a lead role in the screening activity itself. Ideas from senior management may be more likely to proceed into development because they have built implicitly into the reviewing procedures the criteria that favour their ideas, and put ideas from other sources at a disadvantage. In the same vein, ideas from director level are not challenged, or are challenged only superficially, because of the director's political status within the organization. Similarly, product champions with strong personalities may also push ideas through that on reflection, may not have met all the review criteria. Ideas from a customer may be favoured and assumed to be better than an idea from the shop floor, which is discarded without receiving even a cursory evaluation.

People and Politics

Commenting on the social aspects of idea development, Van de Ven (1986) found that 'people develop, carry, react to and modify ideas.

People apply different skills, energy levels and frames of reference (interpretative schemas) to ideas as a result of their backgrounds, experiences and activities.' Allen (1977) also found that 'ideas seem to be communicated primarily by person to person networks.' Pavia (1992) noted that 'it was only through ongoing, often informal discussions among the firm's employees that the firm was able to pin-point the new product concept' and found that ideas gather momentum through informal debate at the front end. Bailetti and Guild (1991) describe the process as the 'shaping of team opinions from heterogeneous and widely disseminated information', acknowledging it as a key success factor in innovation management.

The run-up to screening may also involve a number of sociopolitical issues. Conway and McGuinness (1986) found that 'keeping an idea alive required an ever broadening circle of support', and, in order to develop an idea it had to be 'exposed to the review and criticism of knowledgeable individuals in affected departments.' Van de Ven (1986) also found that:

> *People become attached to ideas over time through a social and political process of pushing and riding ideas into good currency. The social and political dynamics of innovation become paramount as one addresses the energy and commitment that are needed among coalitions of interest groups to develop an innovation.*

In a similar vein, Bower (1970) concludes that 'non executives in a variety of departments exercise judgment and sponsor ideas before those ideas were ready to stand the light of organizational scrutiny.' The political agenda of individuals, motivated by career and other reward systems may well ignore ideas from certain sources in order to promote their own (Pettigrew 1973; and Brown and Ennew, 1975). Such reward systems may well nurture a deep-rooted dislike of failure or discourage experimentation, a key characteristic of innovative behaviour (Pavia, 1991; and Rickards, 1991). This fear of failure, either through accepting a bad idea or rejecting a good idea, has also been noted by other researchers in the field (Rochford and Rudelius, 1992).

Influences on the evaluation of ideas do not come only from within the firm. The firm's relationship with its customers and other stakeholders may affect the idea identification and selection processes. In business-to-business markets, large customers, including powerful distributors, can affect directly which ideas are implemented by the firm, irrespective of any formal processes in place. The significance to the supplier's business of not taking on board a single customer's idea may well outweigh the need to explore other more innovative product development routes over the longer term. Business-to-business relationships are acknowledged as a key part of a firm's innovative activities (Von Hippel, 1978).

Research-Centred Activities

Research is the mechanism by which companies extend and develop their knowledge base. Formal methods for knowledge acquisition, such as scientific experiments or surveys, may be used to obtain reliable knowledge. Technological research-centred activities have been well documented in the literature, particularly in the R&D and technology management areas (Bosomworth and Sage, 1995; Coombs et al., 1987; and Iansiti, 1993). However, this chapter focuses on the knowledge created within the marketing domain to illustrate the issues concerned with the RC process.

Research Activities and Marketing

Market research deals with competitive analysis, forecasting industry and technology trends, market share, market size etc., and the evaluation of marketing performance. Market research tends to provide companies with ideas concerning the appropriate mix of benefits to be included in their product and/or service offering (Johne and Snelson, 1988). Market research provides companies with ideas concerning technology strategy, market positioning and the appropriate identification and segmentation strategy of the customer base amongst others (Kotler, 1988). Both activities are acknowledged to be critical success factors, particularly in the case of new product development (Brooksbank, 1991; Cooper and Kleinschmidt, 1987; Cooper, 1988; Daft and Weick, 1984; Leonard-Barton, 1995; Tidd, 1993; and Wilson and Ghingold, 1987). Despite the benefits that marketing and market intelligence can bring to a firm, little is mentioned of the mechanics of how this benefit is accrued or levered for competitive advantage. For instance, Pavia (1991) concludes that 'the specific mechanisms that enable the firms to identify and satisfy their customer's needs remains unclear.' Similarly, Moenaert and Souder (1990) suggest that 'far less is known about how [market] information is generated and what contingencies might affect this.'

Risk and Uncertainty

One of the major reasons for undertaking market research is to improve or support marketing decision making with a view to reducing marketing risk and uncertainty. This has been termed the 'market research pay off' (Davis, 1993; Zabriskie and Huellmantel, 1994), e.g. by investing in market research the pay-off should be a reduction in risk of a new product failing. Nystrom (1979) has commented on the 'uncertainty gap' where 'perceived uncertainty is assumed to create a tendency for information gathering and processing.' Nystrom highlights a contradiction that lies at the heart of the research pay-off debate when he suggests that more information does not necessarily reduce uncertainty (and thus the perception of risk). Instead it may, through bringing to light information that challenges a company's understanding of a situation (challenging the status quo), produce more uncertainty. In a similar vein, Coombs et al. (1987) make the following comment on innovation:

> [Innovation is] a phenomenon which escapes the neo-classical assumption of perfect information because it creates more uncertainty and more information – firm behaviour can be described as decision making under conditions of imperfect information and uncertainty.

Furthermore, the triggers for undertaking discrete market research activities are sometimes not to attend to the research pay-off, or to the uncertainty gap, but to prove that a particular idea is right in a political sense. External research consultancy is used frequently to bring aspects of credibility and objectivity to what are sometimes ideas for products or services that have been arrived at through more intuitive processes within the firm (Boulding 1994).

The notion that customers know what they want in the future has also received criticism (Walsh et al., 1992) particularly from market research agencies themselves. They suggest that by the time most research emerges it is out of date 'fueling a rear view mirror' approach to marketing (Power, 1993). Lowe and Hunter (1991) comment that 'the end user cannot possibly express an opinion about a totally new product before he has a chance to see it.' The advantage of market research in the early stages of new product development, is seen in its ability to 'identify what the questions and issues are particularly when dealing with the unknown' (Boulding, 1994). However, other commentators pinpoint disadvantages with asking consumers what they want. For instance, Cramp (1994) states 'you won't get novel ideas from market research' and Nishikawa (1989) concludes that 'we can look into the future only by intuition or sensitivity . . . fed by experience.' Chapter 3 reviews market research approaches that address this dilemma.

Research Utilization

Moenaert and Souder (1990) studied how market research agencies were used. They questioned the agencies about the use of their research by clients and found that 'the most important variable determining market researcher's expectations of the use of market research information was interaction . . . (and the effect of interaction) . . . as it affected manager's perceptions of the usefulness of research results.' Mintzberg (1990) comments that 'managers strongly favour verbal media, telephone calls and meetings, over documents.' The literature suggests that individuals will exercise choice in their consumption of knowledge based on how they receive information and the format of the information itself. Moenaert and Souder (1990) concluded that face-to-face communication is very important because it provides feedback between sources, and is very fast and motivational (forces a response). But such transfer of knowledge is usually of a 'fragmentary' nature, is difficult to record and can lead to secondhand processing. Trust was also voiced by respondents in Moenaert's and Souder's study to be critical, as one respondent commented:

Trust is needed in the initial stages of innovation where you commit yourself intellectually. Because in the end, one is actually generating fantasies among adults.

Their study also determined that the usefulness of research was influenced by factors such as 'realism, accuracy, specificity, consistency, completeness and assumption validity,' a long history with the source, similarities in backgrounds (if individuals), and the type of format of information (for example face-to-face is better than a formal report).'

A key skill in research-centred activities is communicating an idea or a new perspective, insight or understanding to others in an organization (Pinto and Pinto, 1990). The problem for organizations is ensuring that tacit knowledge (i.e. highly personal knowledge that is hard to formalize) is turned into communicable knowledge.

Strategy-Centred Activities

The literature suggests that ideas are chosen predominantly where there is a fit with both a firm's strategy ('this is what we would like to do') and its resources ('are we able to do it?') (Hamel and Prahalad, 1993; Hosley et al., 1994, Leonard-Barton, 1992; Prahalad and Hamel, 1990; Prahalad and Hamel, 1991; and Stalk et al., 1992). By the same token, ideas embody certain core technological routes and product/market choices, thus choosing between ideas by implication constitutes strategic choices concerning the future competitiveness of the organization. There is also the possibility that ideas that fall on the periphery or outside the bounds of current strategy, which question the robustness of a proposed strategic direction or vision, may help define strategy itself. In other words, the strategy development process and the nature of ideas that surface within an organization are very closely tied. For instance, certain mixes of ideas may present greater commercial potential in total, compared with the sum of the commercial potential of each idea when evaluated on their own merits. It is not until senior management has a number of ideas to cross-reference that the optimum mix can be identified. Thus, individuals who have a responsibility to develop strategy may be devising strategy based on the mix of ideas that emerge coupled with the existing formal plans and/or strategy of the organization. Strategy can be both emergent and planned (Quinn et al., 1988). Recently, researchers in the field have recognized that movement between strategy and tactical activities have not been explained adequately. Zabriskie and Huellmantel (1994) suggest that there is a gap between the formulation of successful competitive strategies and in implementation ('the concept of strategic planning is strong but managers lack the skills and methods to put their concepts into practice'). Bailetti and Guild (1991) suggest that companies lack the ability to generate operational definitions of new opportunities. They label this the formulation phase where 'activities [are] performed to recognize, shape and evaluate the information necessary for defining opportunities for new products which are both desirable to, and attainable by, the business unit.'

Organizational Learning

The development of a firm's knowledge base is related to its capacity to learn. NPD and innovation demands that an organization learns new things. Thus Baden Fuller (1995) suggests that challenging thinking, unlearning routines and rule breaking are critical aspects of corporate entrepreneurship. These aspects are mirrored in organizational learning,

To initiate learning, competent organizations must possess monitoring mechanisms that can help to anticipate change in both the internal and external environments. These monitoring mechanisms (such as the scanning of published technical reports, scientific meetings, patent reviews , use of consultants, market tests, R&D, team meetings and competitive surveillance) will trigger learning in firms. In order for firms to be able to adopt better learning behaviour, firms 'must first "unlearn" old ways and perceptions by discovering the inadequacies of current approaches and then consciously discarding them' (Meyers and Wileman, 1989). Organizational learning, as opposed to individual learning, is seen to be dependent 'largely on the collective action of individuals to immediate difficulties, imbalances and problems rather than to deliberate planning,' (Meyers and Wilemon, 1989).

Pettigrew and Whipp (1991) recognize 'the fundamentally creative nature of the strategic change process' and that 'the unpredictable nature of these processes had led to the more successful firms to develop learning processes at all levels of the organization.' Their study found that competitive performance was linked to a firm's ability to adapt to major changes in the environment and, by implication, in its level of learning and development of appropriate strategies.

Teams as Learning Mechanisms

Teams are a vital part of a learning organization and can be viewed as 'flexible responsive learning mechanisms' that 'store, retrieve, reinvent, and transfer the contents of [the organization's] knowledge base' (Meyers and Wilemon, 1989). According to Mahoney and Pandian (1992), teams 'experiment, create and integrate new knowledge as they manage the development process.' They continue: 'even if the firm can market its intangible assets effectively, it could not disentangle them from the skills and knowledge of the managerial team. In summary, idiosyncratic physical, human, and intangible resources supply the genetics of firm heterogeneity.' Meyers and Wilemon (1989) conclude:

> *A typical profile for a successful integration team consists of members who possess a T-shaped combination of skills; they are not only experts in specific technical areas but also intimately acquainted with the potential systemic impact of their particular tasks ... while various research groups continue to develop and present new options, it is the integration team that turns new ideas into useful products ... New product development teams are experimenting, creating and integrating new knowledge as they manage the development process ... the success of technological organizations is enhanced by the ability to create, store and retrieve, learning across several new product development teams.*

INTEGRATING IDEA-, RESEARCH- AND STRATEGY-CENTRED ACTIVITIES

As has been illustrated, the integration of these activities occurs in many different places and through many different practices in a firm. Knowledge generated through the iterations between ideas and research mixed with intuition, experience and organizational learning may create a new opinion, an improved understanding or a different product idea or concept (Figure 2.4). Nonaka (1991) suggests:

> *Creating [new] knowledge is not simply a matter of processing objective information. Rather it depends on tapping the tacit and often highly subjective insights, intuitions and hunches of individual employees and making those insights available for testing and use by the company as a whole ... in this respect, the knowledge creating company is as much about ideals as it is about ideas ... it is a way of behaving, indeed a way of being.*

This integration is particularly important at the front end of NPD. Individuals – not just key decision makers but researchers, designers and engineers – may be relying on their local knowledge (that which is most familiar to them) to a greater extent than knowledge they are acquiring from other sources. This may mean that problem solving is unlikely to be objective or rational, but will be prejudiced to the individuals' interpretative schema or frame of reference, with a natural tendency to shy away from new information that could provide the basis for greater innovation. The knowledge transfer process – the collection of informal soft processes by which individuals and groups form local knowledge – becomes critical. Intuition, judgment and experience-based learning becomes paramount over research facts

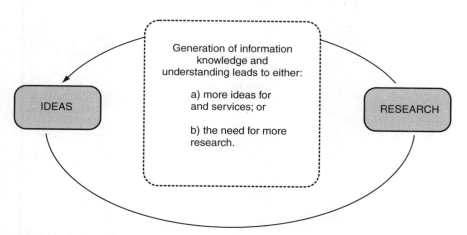

Figure 2.4   Ideas and research activities

collected in what are perceived to be more formalized, discrete and objective research processes. Control of this front end is no longer through formal organizational processes, but via shared mindsets, relationships and vision. A tension arises between the need to be perceived to be thinking logically and rationally by peers, following organizationally agreed processes, versus the desire to follow one's intuition and judgement.

MODELING IDEA-, RESEARCH- AND STRATEGY-CENTRED ACTIVITIES

Research- and idea-centred activities are practices that can occur potentially anywhere in an organization. Organizations acquire information and ideas through both informal and formal means facilitated either by soft or hard processes. Both teams and individuals transform their knowledge bases together with new knowledge to generate concepts for products and services. These may be stand-alone requirements for products, e.g. 'customer X prefers red cars', or

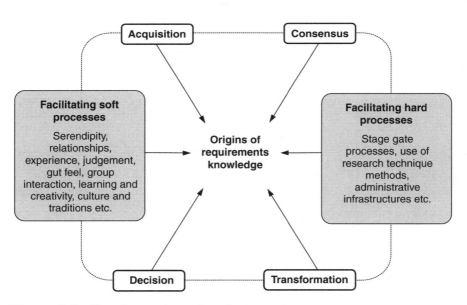

Figure 2.5　Requirements capture framework

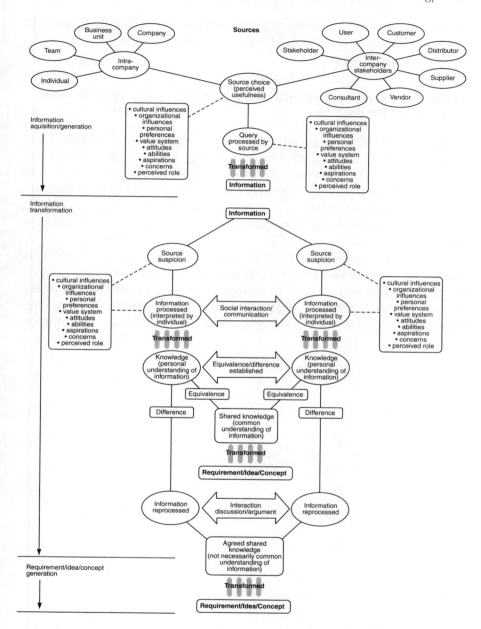

Figure 2.6   A literature-based model of knowledge flows

fully fledged product concept ideas. Because of the iterative nature of the flow, a small amount of information and ideas may lead to more information and ideas.

REQUIREMENTS CAPTURE AS PART OF IDEA DEFINITION AND ENHANCEMENT

Although RC occurs as an ongoing part of organizational activity, and is a result of idea-, research- and strategy-based activities, for the purposes of NPD there is a need to generate requirements to build up the attributes of a product idea. This activity is prone to all the soft and hard processes described in Figure 2.5. However, RC for developing a product concept can also be perceived as a discrete activity (see below).

The process entails three key stages: acquisition of information, its translation into requirements, and decisions about the requirements for the product. Figure 2.6 illustrates this process, showing the RC process-based model of flows in an organization's internal and external environments. (This is described in detail in the introduction to this book).

3 REQUIREMENTS: MARKET RESEARCH TOOLS AND TECHNIQUES

INTRODUCTION

As discussed in Chapters 1 and 2 the requirements to be captured at the front end include all stakeholder requirements. However, the major stakeholders in successful NPD are the customers and end users, therefore this chapter considers the tools and techniques available for identifying their specific requirements.

Customers' expectations are becoming increasingly more demanding. Consumers require high-quality goods and services that are accessible, available and convenient. Manufacturers and retailers are pressurized to meet these expectations and are forced to focus not just on price but on their products' creativity, quality and durability. 'The 90s consumer is hungry for novelty'. (Marketing, 1994) is an apt description. As market needs are difficult to ascertain and customers are unable to articulate their requirements in the abstract, it becomes essential for companies to commit themselves to the continuous development of products (Barczak, 1995). As Tidd (1993) indicates 'incremental innovation demands a deep knowledge of user needs and therefore a close relationship with customers would be beneficial.'

The dynamic marketplace, coupled with the inability of companies to recognize market and technical advances, leaves many companies reacting to consumer needs. A major reason for this can be attributed to inappropriate market research at the early development phases, or lack of user involvement throughout the new product development process, with one consequence being that companies develop products for which there is no market.

Market research has a crucial role to play at the front end of NPD. Market research activities will capture and process information from different sources (e.g. competitors, users, distributors) and this information may influence decisions made about future product requirements. As Pavia (1991) comments, 'recognizing and understanding customer needs and knowledge of the marketplace are essential components of success.'

Although the NPD literature is in common agreement that market research should be used in the early stages of a product's development to help enhance the chances of success, there are examples of successful products that have been developed and launched into the market with little market research. For example, the snack food, 'Phileas Fogg' was launched 'without either qualitative or quantitative research but with manufacturer Derwent Valley Food's conviction that there was a gap in the market for upmarket snacks.' Market research will not replace inspirational product ideas but may help to improve the chances of product success (McKenzie, 1996). As well as carrying out market research, the outcome of the research has to be presented in a form that is readily available and understandable to the product development team. However, there is still significant dissatisfaction from design areas with the type of market information supplied, the quality of this information and the format in which it is delivered (Cooper and Jones, 1994).

Whilst extensive research has been conducted to identify success factors for NPD (Hart, 1992; and Cooper, 1979), there is a significant gap in the literature regarding market research conducted at the front-end stages of the product development process and specifically the identification of user needs and wants. This chapter will consider the role of market research at the front end of NPD and indicate the problems of ascertaining customer needs and wants.

THE ROLE OF MARKET RESEARCH IN NEW PRODUCT DEVELOPMENT

Webster (1993) indicates that unless market research is fed into the front end of NPD, products and services will not be made with the customer requirements in mind:

New products are the lifeblood of any business. Without a good flow of information to the R&D function about needs in the market place and about reaction to initial product concepts, there is a high risk that the products developed will not find acceptance among customers.

Cooper and Kleinschmidt (1988) highlight the benefits of undertaking market research at the front end:

...time spent early on researching the market and developing a product specification is essential to prevent costly and time consuming modifications later.

The use of market research in NPD is concerned with exploring, testing and validating the design and development of new products and the improvement of existing products. With the company's objectives in mind, market research can attempt to verify the latent needs of potential customers. By providing a greater insight into consumers' needs, market research may help to discover fresh ideas for new product development.

As described in Chapter 1, many different models of NPD exist (Kolter, 1980; Booz et al., 1982; Cooper and Kleinschmidt, 1986; Crawford, 1988; and Utterback 1974). Although these may vary, there is consensus that market research can make NPD more effective (Page, 1993). Different market research tools and techniques may be used at different stages of NPD, as shown in Figure 3.1.

Idea Screening

There are numerous internal and external sources that may provide an organization with new product concepts. Pavia (1991) categorized them into formal and informal methods (Table 3.1). Indicating this external sources often relies on customer studies; however, very few studies have been undertaken of the market research tools and techniques most useful to companies at this early phase of NPD, apart from brainstorming techniques (Parnes, 1961). This may be because few companies consider market research as a source of ideas.

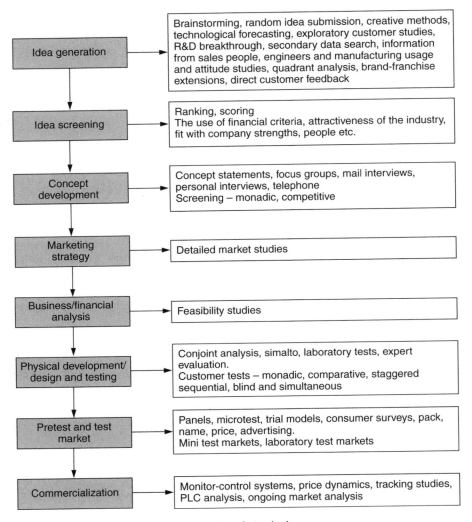

Figure 3.1   Possible market research techniques

As suggested in Marketing (1994):

Whilst market research is important, there is a danger of relying on it too heavily during the creative process . . . you won't get novel ideas from the market research. The consumer can only give you a retrospective response about what they use and how it influences their

Table 3.1 Sources of NPD

	Internal sources of ideas	External sources of ideas
Formal identification process	R&D The strategic plan Organized creativity techniques, e.g. brainstorming	Marketing research New product consultant Industry studies
Informal identification process	Ad hoc ideas from anywhere in the organization Ideas arising during day-to-day meetings and discussions	Customer suggestions Casual conversations Response to competitor products

Source: Pavia (1991), reprinted by permission of Elsevier Science Inc.

> *buying decisions. That's the reason we are called inventors and they are called respondents to market researchers...research can't design a new product for you but it can act as a catalyst and point you in the right direction ...and the newer more revolutionary the product concept the less reliable the research information is going to be.*

There are many formal methods for generating ideas (see Table 3.2). Mathot (1982) has classified idea generation techniques as either systematic analytical techniques (e.g., morphological analysis), associative techniques (such as brainstorming) or analogical techniques (such as synetics). Alternatively, Crawford (1987) has classified idea generation techniques into three types:

1. To identify unmet needs and problems (problem find/solve approach).
2. To modify or improve existing products to create new products (fortuitous scan approach).
3. To find problems and brainstorming to identify possible solutions (problem find/solve approaches).

A growing number of creative techniques have come to the aid of market research for the front end of NPD. Simple creativity techniques for stimulating the imagination and generating ideas are often used in group situations. For example, techniques for imagination may involve wordplay, 'why' questions, or analogies. Idea generation may involve brainstorming, scenarios, morphological analysis, metaphors or mood boards.

Table 3.2   Idea generation techniques

Method	Characteristics	Objectives
Abstraction (progressive abstraction)	Make problem or situation more abstract	Insights into new solutions
Adaptation	Modifying or partial transformation of an existing product for different conditions	Reliable solution for new conditions
Aggregation	Combination of product characteristics into a single product, or of functions of a number of products into one product	New properties, simplified structure
Analysis of properties (attribute listing)	Thorough analysis of every property of the product	Improvement of an existing product
Application	Application of an existing product for new functions	Application of a proven product to new areas of use
Attribute-based discriminant analysis (PREFMAP)	Market segments developed on basis of brand preferences, geometric representation developed by discriminant analysis from brand's effective attributes, then mapped and analysed	Market structure generated and searched for new product opportunities
Brainstorming	Collect ideas in freewheeling discussion without criticism	Find many new ideas
Combinations with interactions	Combining of a product or properties to obtain new and more complicated effects	Derive new solutions from existing products
Critical path network	Graphic representation and activities and their duration	Create an overview of the sequence and timing and find the critical path opportunities
Descartes	Four principles, criticism, division, ordering, create overview	Correctness and effectiveness of thought process stimulates ideas

Method	Characteristics	Objectives
Dimensional investigation	Technical and economic properties of the product brought together into a mathematical relationship and extreme values found	Find optimal solution on product properties
Division of totality	Tactical procedure based on division of a whole concept or problem into component parts	Create overview, generate partial solutions
Evaluation	Find technical and economic valuation by point counting	Find best variant among a few
Experimentation	By measuring and testing, obtain desired values	Determination of product
Incubation	After thorough preparation of the problem, take a break	Find ideas by intuition

Source: Rochford (1991).

Table 3.3   Idea screening techniques

Ranking
Checklists
Scoring models
Network models
Attribute-based analysis
Numerical weighting methods
Line profiles
Block profiles
Idea sort
Profitability index method

The screening of product ideas is also important in developing products to enable resources to be assigned to the most promising product ideas, while discarding the least promising. There are a number of techniques that allow companies to undertake this activity. Although not solely the demand of market research, they are frequently used by this function and are often referred to in the corresponding literature. Idea screening techniques are shown in Table 3.3.

Screening techniques can identify ideas for further development. Although the literature does indicate numerous formal methods for generating ideas and screening, the extent to which companies actually use such techniques at the front end of product development remains largely unexplored.

Concept Development and Testing

The concept development phase of the product development process may involve market research activity, including identifying customer needs to refining the concept specifications. The product concept needs to be translated into a preliminary product design. Models may be used to test the functions of the product concept. This step may also entail the construction of mock-ups. Full- or limited-scale models may be used to test attributes or buyer reaction, or simply to provide a visual representation of the proposed product.

At the early phase of concept development, many techniques may be applied to provide information about the way consumers will react to a new product and their likely acceptance and appeal of the concept.

To refine concept specifications (e.g. attributes, functions) techniques such as conjoint analysis and laboratory tests may be used to ensure the most important or unique aspects of the product relate to consumer preferences. Davis (1993) suggests that when undertaking concept testing, 'the concept should be as close as possible to the final one to be presented.'

Marketing Strategy

In the development of marketing strategy, a detailed study of the market may be undertaken to ensure that a market exists for the product. Detailed desk research may be conducted to gather information related to the marketplace, market sector, industry characteristics, competitors etc.

Business Analysis

Feasibility studies may be undertaken using models and methods to predict sales forecasts. The concept is evaluated against business and market objectives and goals of the company. This frequently leads to a no/go decision prior to the product development.

Product Development and Testing Pretest Models and Test Markets

After business analysis, a more detailed product design and proto-types may be created. Essentially, this is testing the marketing mix of a new product to a limited geographical market. Techniques cited in the literature include the use of diary, panels and laboratory test and test marketing (Urban and Hauser, 1993).

Commercialization

Once the product has been launched into the marketplace, marketing and market research may track the product to check how the product is selling, perceived by customers, etc.

Davis (1993) has identified eight market research lessons to facilitate successful NPD:

1. Use market research to improve decision making.
2. Have a business strategy and market research plan for discovering strong ideas.
3. Use a well-founded screening approach to identify ideas for further development.
4. Develop and test concepts before going to full-scale product development.
5. Start forecasting sales and profitability at concept stage.
6. Use market research to refine the elements of the product and marketing mix.
7. Use test markets if possible to prevent a disaster.
8. Do not make last-minute changes that have not been qualified.

Whilst it is recognized that market research is important for effective NPD, the focus of the research to date has been on identifying where market research fits into NPD in a general way. The concern of this chapter is the role of market research at the front end of NPD. The positive and negative benefits of using market research are discussed next, before reporting on three examples of the approaches used for NPD for consumer goods.

ISSUES FOR MARKET RESEARCH AT THE FRONT END OF NEW PRODUCT DEVELOPMENT

Although the literature is consistent with the view that market research is important for NPD, a number of problems may be associated with its use.

Irrelevant and Unreliable Information

If market research information is not unreliable, then the product development team may be given inappropriate briefs. Concepts may then be developed with the belief that there is a real need for the product in the market. Consequently, resources, money and time may be wasted on NPD to develop a concept, which, when tested, shows only that the market research was wrong.

Activities are Undertaken in Form Only

> *A form of best practice may be followed while content is largely ignored.*
>
> Brown and Ennew, 1995

The fact that a market research activity has been carried out does not mean to say that the actual substance of market research has been recognized by management and decision makers within an organization. As Brown and Ennew (1995) suggest, 'the simple observation that an activity [market research] has been carried out does not, itself, ensure that the implications/substance of that activity has been fully appreciated.'

Brown and Ennew present an NPD case study of a new children's confectionery product. To summarize the case, research was conducted through a market research agency to assess market size, competition, design, packaging, price and distribution. The results proved disappointing and 'the project team attached little weight to these results.' Another agency was commissioned, which also revealed negative aspects associated with the product. Despite much uncertainty surrounding the product, management confidence in the product was high. Therefore, resources were put into developing the product further. Management later dropped a planned TV test and a national campaign started immediately. Although sales were in excess of forecasts, the same was true of costs. This case represents an example of the use of research as a rite of passage for the project to continue regardless, while acceptinbg only favourable results from the research, and withholding and filtering the negative findings of the research.

Conflicting Perceptions

Conflicting perceptions of researchers and managers may be present within an organization or between an organization and its agency. This may be because researchers are seeking to provide new and hitherto unknown directions. Researchers prefer to produce new insights rather than verifying existing information, and therefore they may react positively to uncertainty, whilst managers are attempting to reduce uncertainty. Therefore, managers may not be at ease with results that conflict with their expectations.

Confirming Expectations

> *Sometimes the real purpose of doing market research is to prove we are right . . .*
>
> Vinten, 1994

Management may use market research to validate and confirm decisions already decided.

In attempting to validate decisions, management may attempt to control research results to justify themselves. As Bean (quoted in Boulding, 1994) believes:

> *One of the malaise's of British management is the notion that there is a need to control the outcome of research and only investigate these areas of decision making process that present straightforward evidence.*

Management may manipulate results with the intention to further personal gains, such as promotion within an organization. Kinnear and Taylor (1991) highlight:

Knowledge gained through personal experience and observation can be biased by our selective perception of reality so distorting facts to benefit personal objectives and to confirm with existing attitudes.

Scapegoat for Wrong Decisions

Market research may be used as a scapegoat for wrong decisions. Managers can, and do, make decisions regardless of market research. Davis (1993) suggests 'whilst companies still may conduct a considerable amount of market and consumer research, this may not be fully exploited in ultimate product decisions. Too often product managers and top managers still base their product decisions on instinct, or on reactions to their competition.'

The problems associated with market research for NPD are concerned mainly with the acceptance of results by management and their opinions towards the usefulness of market research. However, although market research does have problems, these are not always associated with the way it is conducted; rather, these problems may arise because management have not recognized the importance of market research. This is perhaps due to the ignorance of managers as they feel they 'know the market too well to need market research' (Walsh et al., 1992).

Capturing User Needs

Capturing user needs may prove beneficial to an organization; however there are a number of problems associated with capturing requirements in NPD. When undertaking research, users do not know what they want in the abstract as Ireland and Johnson (1995) suggest:

Consumers are certainly the most qualified customers on their current lives, but not necessarily reliable authorities on their future lives ... Because people can not reliably imagine how they will use a new product, their response to questions is likely to be unreliable.

Lowe and Hunter (1991) also highlight this: 'The end users cannot possibly express useful opinions about a totally new product before she/he has a chance to see it.'

When attempting to capture user needs, innovation and technology may be too far ahead for customers to even envisage such products. Woudhuysen (1994) stresses this by commenting:

> *Tomorrow's new information technology based products and services are very hard to subject to market research. Ask most people whether they would like this or that gadget or service and the answers are unlikely to be too revealing.*

The ultimate test of NPD success or otherwise is essentially the response of the end user. Therefore, users may be viewed as important for NPD. As Walsh et al. (1992) suggests, 'market research does not tell you what the product needs, to do this information is required from the user.' This leads the authors to postulate that end users should be involved in market research throughout the duration of the NPD process. The front end of product development is of particular interest because capturing consumer requirements is crucial for NPD, and capturing user needs through market research may reduce the risk of product failure:

> *Market research enables producers of goods and services to design and deliver their products according to the informed preferences of the final consumer and so reduces the risk of costly production mistakes being made . . .*
>
> Moore and Pessemier, 1993

However, Leonard-Barton (1991) believes that the identification of needs does not in itself guarantee a successful marketing strategy, although it is a logical first step in the right direction:

> *Merely increasing emphasis on market research in itself does not lead to better understanding of user needs and a higher probability of product success.*

COMPANY EXAMPLE: A NEW WALL COVERING

Introduction to the Idea

The market research agency was approached by a wallpaper manufacturer to research a new wall covering that was being developed in their R&D department. The idea was of a wall covering that could be applied directly on to a wall without having to use paste. The research process is shown in Figure 3.2.

Gathering Background Information and Proposal

Firstly, background information was collected about the client, the competition, its existing products and the market trends for wall covering. The agency then drew up a research proposal as to what they believed should be addressed. Within this proposal, a plan of the research stages was indicated. However, the company was sceptical about the benefits of the research process, due to the time and costs involved. The agency therefore focused the research on a step-by-step approach. As the market research agency commented, 'the process is not something that can be carved in stone.'

Sampling the Target Market

Once the client had agreed to proceed with stage one of the research, the market research agency took a sample of the target market (DIY enthusiasts) to check that there was a potential market for the concept.

Developing the Concept

After the client and the agency took a decision to go ahead with the project, a number of creative groups were set up to develop the concept further. These creative groups focused on understanding the motivations behind two sets of influencers, the user and the buyer. Within these groups, stimulus material, such as bubble drawings and collage boards, was used as well as projective techniques, such as associations.

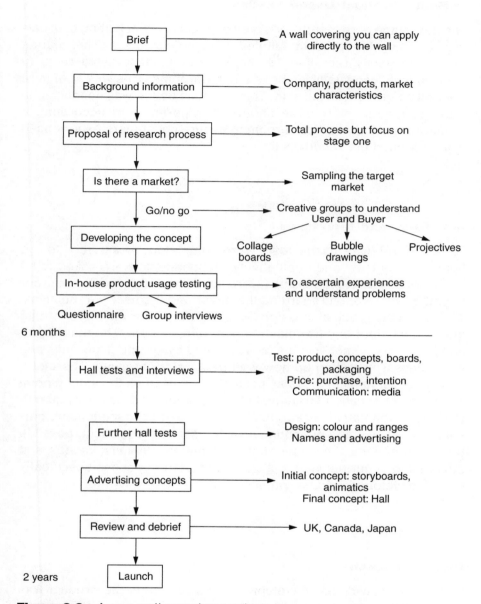

Figure 3.2 A new wall covering product

In-House Product Usage Testing

The next stage of research consisted of initial product testing to ascertain whether the product fulfilled a customer need. The market research agency recruited 100 households to decorate a room in their houses, especially kitchens and bathrooms. This was to ensure the wall covering was durable. This in-house usage was conducted in order to gather information about the experience of decorating a whole, rather than part of, a room to ensure consumers experienced cutting around the window sills.

Hall Tests and Interviews

Once the in-house usage tests were completed, these were tested both quantitatively and qualitatively. Respondents were asked to fill in a questionnaire, then groups were conducted with couples in order to gather information regarding the buyer and the user perspectives. The aim of the group discussions was to gather information regarding the pain barriers and traumas of decorating a room. The main problem for the consumer was the mess created by stripping the walls and not necessarily putting up new wall paper straight away. Therefore, this insight of as little mess as possible was used as the selling point of the communication strategy. Following another iteration of quantitative and qualitative research, hall tests were conducted using personal interviews and questionnaires to assess the product, possible prices, communications, purchase intentions, designs, names and advertising. A further hall test was conducted to assess specifically further developed colours, ranges, advertising and names.

Product Launch

Following the two-year development and research, the product was launched successfully in DIY superstores and the product idea was also sold to retailers to distribute their own brand.

TOOLS AND TECHNIQUES FOR IDENTIFYING NEW PRODUCT DEVELOPMENT

Research undertaken by the authors and their team involved a survey of a sample of research agencies. It was possible to build up a table of the tools and techniques commonly used for different aspects of consumer research for NPD. Overall, it was clear that the agencies focus on qualitative approaches at the front end of NPD and the choice of technique was most often related to the experience of the researchers involved, as illustrated by the quotations from researchers below.

The tools and techniques identified as used by market research agencies at different stages of a concept's early development are described here and are summarized in Table 3.4. Techniques to identify ideas may be researched; alternatively, a client may already have an idea or concept to be researched. In this case an agency may be used to identify, for example, an idea's opportunity within different markets.

> Clients are saying 'I have got this idea' and draw it up on the blackboard ... where do we market this, is there a market for this and where is the best market for this, what sort of size, shape and specification should it have in that marketplace?
>
> *Market researcher*

Desk Research

The importance of desk research is often overlooked: 'We do not use existing data enough,' claims one respondent. However, desk research is a good starting point that can help identify new opportunities available in an existing market; a participant stated that:

> We will find out what the trends are, how things are changing, how the market is structured, whether there are any gaps and what we can create.

Table 3.4 Tools and techniques used by eight market research agencies

P.D Process	Company 1	Company 2	Company 3	Company 4	Company 5	Company 6	Company 7	Company 8
Desk research		Existing info/products				Market	Trend/market pointer/analysis Market mapping	Gap analysis/tracking/mapping
Segmentation	Industry sector/Company size/location/ownership	Decisions/attitudes/values/needs/beliefs	Focus groups	Omnibus		Groups		
Idea generation	Focus groups/interviews		Existing products	Group collage/Boards/Bubble drawings		Home visits/Brainstorming/videos	Brainstorming with existing brands/stimulus Scenarios/Headlines	Brainstorming
Screen idea		Criterion						Screen test
Build attributes	Conjoint analysis	Groups/depths	Conjoint analysis	Simalto/Simalto Plus			Brand audit/association/personification	
Develop concept further	Observation/Focus groups	Statements/facilitation/groups	Obituaries/personification/Kelly triads/mood boards		Dialectics/synergies/depths/hall	Two-chair work Creative groups		Panel of users
Screen concept	Swot/Acumen	Screen test						
Test product/price/communications		Paired depths/projectives	Conjoint analysis Gabor Grainger	Halls	Questionnaires/hall/focus groups	Groups/Brainstorming	Halls/home Placement/phone recall	Group discussion

Consumer Trends Review

This type of desk research involves looking at international behaviour and attitudes and how appropriate these are to the 1990s across countries to a greater and lesser extent. A number of consumer trends, e.g. escapism, individualism and greening, are identified from different information sources that are continually updating and evolving. Such trend reviews help in the generation of ideas at a qualitative stage in the development of concepts as one of the market researchers explained:

> We would use these as a springboard to give a pattern of brainstorming with the client. Say think about the fact people live busy lives . . .

Pointer Market Analysis

Pointer market analysis involves desk research that is looking at what is happening in particular regions, e.g. looking to new developments in the USA. This was recognized by one market research company as 'incredibly useful' to help identify new opportunities that may be transferred to markets in the UK.

Parallel Market Analysis

Undertaking desk research to look at related markets, this involves identifying opportunities in similar markets to the clients. For example, looking at trends in the drinks market when developing a new product in the savoury snacks market.

Competitor Review

This will involve finding out what the client's competitors are doing by watching the marketplace to keep up to date with new developments.

Market Mapping

This involves mapping all products in the marketplace to identify how they fit together. This allows the agency to compare against other brands in the market and to identify any gaps or potential gaps in the market.

Existing Company Products and Brands

This desk research may also include information on a brand's history with a detailed evaluation of the brand to research how brands are perceived. This may involve assessing whether there is any baggage associated with the brand or whether there is a parent or sister brand. A researcher explained:

> *Without knowing if the brand had a personality, we could not go into the next stage of generating new ideas.*

Group Discussion

This consists of a group of about 8 to 12 people who may have been chosen specifically or at random to take part in a discussion. This section will show how research agencies conduct groups and use different tools to generate ideas.

Advantages

The advantage of group discussions over other research techniques was highlighted by one interviewee:

> *Groups are brilliant for chucking around ideas and growing them. You do not get that in a one-to-one interview.*

Another respondent felt it was the interaction between different people that is needed more specifically for product development work:

> *The advantage of groups is if you are looking at something in the future like product development or reactions to a specific concept, the interaction between the group is great.*

Ways of Conducting Groups

Groups can be conducted by researchers in various ways; one method was explained by a market researcher. The dialectic approach to group discussions may be used to generate feelings and motivations around a concept. This involves 'deliberately putting two opposite views together [in one group] to challenge each other... different perceptions and different psychological desires merge out of this interface.' An example may be putting together people who had and had not visited a destination to create opposing views as to why one should or should not visit the location.

However, it is important to take into consideration that certain groups of people may not mix well in a group situation, proving to be less effective than expected as a respondent explained:

> *You need to take into account that men and women do not mix well in groups, nor old and young... it is better to have homogeneous groups. People do argue: if you have different people in a group it is more creative and innovative but it is more unmanageable and you can not analyse what was important*

Group Game Playing

Brainstorming can take place in-house to generate simple concepts. One company undertook brainstorming in-house with their clients: 'We may do a series of workshops with senior people. Trying to float options to look at where opportunities lie. For generating opportunities and product ideas you need creativity.' Alternatively, agencies may generate concepts externally with consumers, or use both methods.

For the generation of concept ideas, an informal process is important to explore possible avenues and identify opportunities in the market. Therefore, it is crucial to have an open minded approach and to not get tunnel visioned, as one interviewee explained:

> *You have to be careful, the first rule of NPD is do not have an opinion, be open minded*

Another respondent felt this informality can foster imagination and creativity:

> *Other colleges like to be sophisticated... but I get lots of stuff in and let customers throw it out so you can move on to the elements that work... It can be distracting to go into prompt detail such as typeface*

or shape at this point so it is still open and throwing different things into the mix.

Group game playing can be conducted in many ways and numerous stimuli may be used as described below. One company has widened the ability of game playing to include various techniques borrowed from psychotherapy. As a respondent explained, the use of one technique called 'two-chair work' was used in the development of a food product.

> *We employ a psychotherapist to invent new games and techniques. For example, 'two-chair work,' where one principle of psychotherapy is that we have different sub personalities ... a psychotherapist will say 'put the scared side in that chair and speak from that chair' ... It is about getting consumers to live and experience things ... We might have consumers for a day and a half just playing games.*

Creative Tools for Gathering Ideas

The use of techniques by research agencies developed for creativity purposes are prominent in a group situation or game playing.

Projective techniques are those which attempt to get the respondent to get feelings and behaviours that relate to the new product. There are numerous creativity tools and techniques that can be drawn upon by researchers. The findings reported six alternatives used by different agencies:

1. *Statements*   The client or agency may develop a number of statements, e.g. 'Doctors recommend you eat a bar of chocolate for breakfast everyday' to attempt to get consumers to think around the subject, be intrigued and suggest the wider implications that this may have.
2. *Scenarios*   Scenarios attempt to get your respondent to imagine they are in a specific situation and to look ahead to what may possibly happen. For example, getting consumers to imagine

what would happen in an impossible dream or a nightmare scenario.

3. *Headlines*   Similar to statements, headlines get consumers thinking around subjects and to comment on specific topics. For example, the headline. 'Gerbeco wins international award for innovative new drink' allowed the agency to explore what that would be and why the drink was award-winning.

4. *Obituaries*   This may involve getting consumers to relate a concept or product to a deceased person; e.g. to write an obituary for the type of person they feel may relate to a product.

5. *Associations*   This involves consumers associating a brand or product with something else. For example, asking 'What animal does this brand represent?' or 'What kind of underwear would this be?'

6. *Personification*   This is also similar to associations although you attempt to relate the product by associating it with a person. For instance, 'What celebrity sums up the brand? Is it lively, young, dynamic, old, fashionable?'

Visual stimuli and the use of creative drawings may be used for generating ideas in a group/game playing situation. One respondent believes that 'it is difficult for consumers to articulate what they want but easy to draw it.'

The most commonly used visual stimuli are mood boards. Less common are bubble drawings, story boards and collage boards, but all were identified for generating concept ideas by various companies. One company used bubble drawings and mood boards in the development of concepts for a new wall covering product, as outlined in Figure 3.2. The use of visual stimuli enables a concept to look more tangible while helping to clarify and refine a concept idea.

Another company has taken the use of visual stimuli in groups even further, as the partner explains when undertaking work for a haircare client company: '[The agency] had a welder welding things in the meeting to look at structure; a potter showing how to shape and mould; a film and make up person showing the tricks of the trade; and the beauty editor of *Cosmopolitan* . . . offering their views.' This enables the consumer, the client and the various professionals to mix, give their opinions and bounce ideas around.

Processes and Techniques for Refining Concepts

> *It may take several stages before you feel something [a concept] is worth testing further.*
>
> Market researcher

The process of developing concepts further is a narrowing one to explore possible concept options. As a respondent suggests:

> *You may get a client with a concept but it may end up as a different concept ... [or] ... in some cases you may end up with nothing, because there is no market gap .... There are various points where we are throwing out things in the process, discarding and limiting down.*

Initially, a concept needs to be explored thoroughly to assess whether the idea or product lives up to the subconscious criteria held in consumer's minds. The process of identifying the right concept may take a number of iterations to filter out the specifics of a concept, including exploring concept names, propositions, and packaging elements. One respondent suggests that when exploring concepts in a group situation it should be 'like a video, if you get a bit wrong [it is best to] change it there and try it again.'

One interviewee recognized the importance of identifying possible concepts through a process called concept capture. This is a type of future-orientated audit by normative evaluation used to identify concept names, product features, potential consumers, styling issues, competitive advantages, delivery mechanisms and resource implications. Concept generation involved the use of focus groups to identify consumer perceptions using personification, user imagery and associations. From the research findings, broad concept statements and propositions could be identified to allow the agency to develop a more refined concept brief. Further qualitative concept development research was undertaken to look more closely at the concepts generated to enable more detailed positioning options. Such options were then taken to further focus groups to identify the most promising option to take to a quantitative research stage, which involved hall tests, home placement and telephone interviewing techniques to validate and test more rigorously the findings of the qualitative research.

Home Visits and In-House Testing

In-house placements with products enable the product to be used by consumers in familiar surroundings. This technique provides insight into the problems consumers experience and the aspects that need enhancing further. A variation of this technique was used by one interviewee who states:

> *I recruited about 20 people and hired a street. I am going to wander down the street with the staff from a technical department of a company and consumers are going to cook their products, try them and use them. We are going to go into all the homes on the street and chat to people and ask them to show us how they used the product.*

This technique also allows for observation. Other in-house placements may last for a week, and respondents will be asked to fill in a questionnaire or attend a group discussion or interview following this period. This process was used in the case of the wallpaper (Figure 3.2) to capture respondents' specific grievances, likes and overall perspectives of the product.

Conjoint Analysis

Conjoint analysis may be used by agencies to identify and build a set of attributes around a product concept. As one company explained, the purpose of conjoint analysis is 'to look at product attributes and characteristics of a product that a company should aim for in a development programme.' The identification of attributes may be carried out qualitatively at an earlier level to understand particular attributes. As the concept is developed further, importance ratings are converted into utility scores to identify where opportunities lie and their importance as differentiators in the marketplace.

Another respondent highlighted that conjoint analysis enables the agency to 'look at the influence of various attributes and willingness to buy due to inherent attractiveness. What is important, how important are certain attributes and preference of those for a particular person.'

Simultaneous Multi-Attribute Trade-Off

Simultaneous multi-attribute trade-off (Simalto) is based on a trade-off principle to look at the multiplicity of attributes a product concept may have. One market researcher noted that her company 'applies a model called Simalto Plus which pulls together issues of importance, expectation, perceptions and issues of trade off to prioritize improvements...Simalto can be used equally well in generating new products, as it can actually identify the actual elements of a product. It is used a lot in NPD for cars, airlines, computers.'

Screening and Testing the Concept

> *You should not formalize the front end because generating ideas has to be creative; if you close down too early you are not going to get wacky ideas...It is vetting the ideas that is crucial because you do not want to lose any good ideas.*
>
> Market researcher

Once concepts have been developed further, research may move to a quantitative stage to screen and identify the most promising concepts. Refining the aspects of the product, such as positioning, pack design, pricing and advertising may follow such screening. Screening is a continual process throughout the up-front stages of a development programme, as one respondent describes:

> *There are various points where we are throwing things out in the process, discarding and limiting down. In some cases you may end up with nothing.*

Although the research executive explained that the company does have a more formal quantitative technique used for this purpose:

> *We have a quick method of screening down concepts...It is a quantitative method to see the winners and losers called Criterion.*

Once concepts have been screened, the remaining promising concepts are taken to a further stage. Techniques that may be used at this stage may include hall tests to test and validate a number of elements. For example, price may be tested by using monadic price testing or brand price trade-off in a hall situation. Techniques for researching advertising in hall tests included, for example, story boards and animatics.

WHICH TECHNIQUES WHERE?

The blend of both qualitative and quantitative techniques enable agencies to examine different aspects of problems related to product development. An agency can call upon a battery of techniques useful to carry out research. Many companies specialize in certain techniques, such as conjoint analysis, while others may simply apply different techniques to different situations.

It is evident that many techniques, e.g. groups, can be used for a number of purposes from idea generation to testing and validating the end product. It is the way the technique is carried out that changes. This will depend on the research objectives and stage of development. At the predevelopment stage of product development (i.e. idea generation), the agency may feel that the client will benefit from using creativity techniques or psychotherapy techniques to grasp a deeper understanding of a particluar area. A researcher said: 'One of our beliefs is when you are innovating you need to look at things in a new way. If you just talk to consumers, they never give you the answer.' When generating ideas, creativity techniques are not always applicable or relevant, however; one company prefer to use a simplistic approach to conduct this: 'My philosophy is "keep it simple" rather than getting too sophisticated ... otherwise consumers ... do not point you in the right direction.' Another respondent also highlighted the point that techniques must be relevant and applicable:

> There is no point getting a respondent to go through mind-blowing creative techniques if you feel you have got what you need by asking a simple question.

Such techniques are available however and are used by many agencies: 'There are really interesting creative techniques, sophisticated and psychological techniques that nobody uses, it is all informal.'

Techniques are used at the discretion of the researcher and even the extent to which they favour a technique: One researcher believes 'there is no rule of thumb, other than what feels right for the sort of people you are talking to.'

The UK managing director at one company explains:

> *The head of our qualitative unit here is a renowned academic in this area but you only see them running groups or running set interviews and it looks the same as everything else. What they bring to it is a better understanding of what is going on in people's minds so they can interpret better. I think qualitative researchers use the same box of techniques.*

Techniques can, and are, applied across different stages of a product's development. However, there is an overriding concern to get away from the professional response. The consideration of cost must be accounted for, especially for smaller companies, as one respondent suggests: 'If there is a choice of two or three techniques, what are the costs involved with each?'

Agencies commonly arrange projects around teams who have no specialist area (e.g. consumer, high-technology etc.). This allows techniques to be translated across different industries, as seen in the majority of agencies. The development of market research personnel in agencies has improved by recruiting agency and client personnel to generate a mixture of skills across teams. It is these teams that have the ability to create the time, which clients do not have, for good marketing thinking.

Client Relationship

Building the Relationship

> *Clients get the suppliers they deserve and vice versa...It is not the nature of the research that changes; it is the nature of the client–agency relationship.*
>
> > Respondent from market company

The interviews in our research indicated an overwhelming apprecia-
tion of the importance of establishing a rapport early on in the client–
agency relationship. In the example of the wall covering, it was evident that the briefing and proposal stages of the programme gave
both agency and client the opportunity to establish fundamental
aspects of the relationship. This may involve how the agency and
client perceive the problem; one respondent suggests '70 per cent
of the time, we do not work on the given brief; if clients do not think
our angle on the problem is right we feel it is better they do not work
with us . . . so it is a self-selecting process.'

This relationship may build gradually through collaboration with the
client and checking the progress and direction of the development
project. An interviewee recognizes this as a process of 'almost
debriefing all the way through.' Two respondents appreciate that
clients should be constantly involved in all aspects of the project:

> As an external resource we need to keep constantly in touch with the
> client and that is where a lot of agencies go wrong. They just go off
> and do it . . . people need to know how you have got where you have
> got to and get involved in the various stages and so they are in the
> same direction.

> A lot of market research companies say 'There is your consumer
> group and now it is up to you.' You need to get clients to engage in
> the thought process.

Another interviewee suggests market research agencies are not
always considered a valuable resource: 'Sometimes there is a feeling
of arrogance or "We could have thought of that, but thought we would
pay you to do it," – a reticence which can make a working relationship
difficult.'

Managing the Relationship

Through the process and development of the research programme,
the client relationship has to be managed carefully. One example of
managing this relationship may be in the process of debriefing the
client. Differing approaches to this were found, for example, running a
workshop for their clients to get the project group to take on board and

champion the concept or idea. The research executive explains 'I step out and let the client get on with it . . . We can only advise, not say this is what you must do.' Another company have devised a three-day session to enable marketing and technical people 'who have emotional ties' to hand over the product concept to other departments to undertake the final communications, design etc. of the product.

Integrating Client and Customer

Getting the client to recognize the importance of the end user in the development of a client's product is crucial. Therefore, as one respondent explained, 'You are training the client as your customer as well.' Market research agencies provide the stimulus and direction for companies to get close to their customers and live as they would, therefore helping the client deliver a product that customers want while fulfilling a need (as opposed to a product the company wants to give the consumer). One company have a vision of how clients should be aiming to integrate consumers into their culture:

> *Our dream . . . every brand manager will think as though he/she has a settee full of consumers and every time he/she does anything asks what they think . . . we would like every board to have a director of consumers.*

CONCLUSIONS

A diversity of the market research activities are undertaken by research agencies to develop new products. Qualitative research is used primarily to conduct research for the early stages of product development.

Section Two of this book illustrates, through case studies, how companies have used various processes for RC and requirements management throughout the NPD process.

SECTION TWO
Capturing and Managing Requirements Capture in Practice

4

INTRODUCTION TO THE CASE STUDIES

In this section, RC management of companies from a range of industries – automotive, IT, healthcare, construction – is examined in detail. Whilst the companies face different problems, they carry out similar activities to identify the key requirements to build into new and modified products. Talking to customers, working with suppliers and formulating cross-disciplinary product development teams are evident. However, their ability to manage requirements varies.

Colossus is a global IT company that produces business and consumer products and operates in every part of the world. Despite its success, the company was worried about becoming complacent. It wanted to maintain a leading position through the creation of exciting products that were technically advanced. Creativity was a problem. A review of product development activities and business processes was undertaken and from this, it was decided to develop a creative think tank that would drive innovation throughout all the business divisions. The think tank would be comprised of people that had distinctive abilities, skills and competencies, for example engineers with a logical perspective, designers with a gut feel approach, etc. These people would dabble and produce a constant stream of ideas. The ideas would be captured on a A4 sheet of paper and then presented to the business divisions. If they liked the ideas, they would develop this further. No databank of ideas would be set up to store promising ideas. The company believed that if the ideas were effective, then they would be bubble up again, possibly at a more appropriate time.

Vantage is a world-beating car company. The company has a formal process for requirements management, which is carried through each phase of the product development process until it is essential to freeze this, in order to tool-up and produce the cars. Market research is a driver in the process. Concepts are defined and tested for the first two years of the process. Once the concept fits with target customer needs and the distributors have fed into the process, then the company moves into detailed design. The concept has to fit with the business needs of the company and its corporate plan. Once it does so, then the concept is signed off. This process is one of focus, refinement and checking to make sure that nothing silly can happen, and to reduce risk and cost of failure.

Bandage is a successful healthcare company with its origins in the UK. Over the past decade, the company has undergone phenomenal growth, mainly through acquisition. It has a range of leading edge branded products for over-the-counter purchase and also professional products for healthcare professionals. The company has a product development process with inputs from marketing, technical, finance and production. This has been an effective approach. However, with the company's growth, it has under-utilized its manufacturing capability and so is keen to develop new products. Its approach to product development is under review. RC and requirements management are both aspects that could offer improvements.

Construct is a global construction company that manufactures tools. A few years ago, changes in European heath and safety laws opened up new market opportunities in this very traditional industry. Innovation management was not a strength of the company – no new innovations had occurred in the company's market for over 40 years. The European headquarters of the company decided to seize this opportunity and so a product development team was formed by the European marketing director. The team had four members with backgrounds in engineering design, production, marketing and systems. A close relationship was established with a product design company, who quickly became inculcated into the team. The start of the project was to identify requirements for the innovative product.

BACKGROUND

Colossus Computing plc is a multinational IT company. It is divided into three main business sectors: Technologies, Services and Industrial. Within these three areas are ten distinct business divisions, each of which operate on a European or global basis. Each division pursues its own business-specific strategies, and has the resources necessary to develop its business, including channels of distribution, staff, partnerships and financial resources. In the wider context, sectors intertrade, have a common approach to business and share a common vision.

Focus of Study

The focus of the research was on the Colossus Operations division within the Technologies business sector, for three reasons. Firstly, Operations is the fastest growing division of Colossus Computing, generating both new products and services, and spinning them off to build new businesses within the division. Secondly, the division's focus on systems integration and service provision led to the conclusion that it is extremely likely to conduct RC of some sort, and would be relevant to our research. Finally, of the 28 sites at which Colossus Operations has more than five people working, 24 are in the UK.

Within the Colossus Operations division, investigation was concentrated on the Technology Projects subdivision. Technology Projects is responsible for the development of technologies and provision of ideas, concepts, products and systems that can ultimately be utilized by other parts of the Colossus Operations division and Colossus Computing, and/or grown into new businesses. As the research project is looking primarily at RC activities during the front end of product

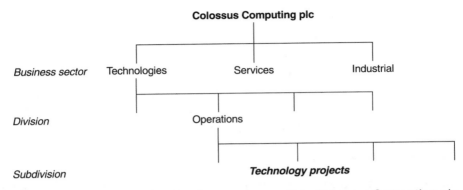

Figure 5.1   Position of technology projects within Colossus Computing plc

development, Technology Projects was considered a relevant focus for study. The position of Technology Projects in the structure of Colossus Computing is shown in Figure 5.1.

Colossus Computing and Requirements Capture

Since the mid-1980s, Colossus Computing has shifted its business focus from hardware manufacture to service provision, and it would seem sensible to suggest that this might have affected the company's activities during product development. The company's aim, as the mission statement puts it, 'to improve the performance and profitability of our customers' businesses,' requires that there is a considerable understanding of exactly how a customer's business operates, and what they would classify as an improvement. How Colossus Computing achieves this level of understanding is obviously relevant to RC. The company would seem to be committed to much of what constitutes RC (i.e. the collection of stakeholder information, its analysis, and the use of this information to generate an appropriate solution), as the company literature states:

> *Colossus Computing's fundamental principle has been to do real things with real users, to pilot and to experiment. Direct consumer feedback ensures that what Colossus Computing does is meaningful and useful, and that a core body of experience and skill is built within the new . . . markets.*

Technology Projects

Nearly all of the divisions and subdivisions of Colossus, with the exception of Technology Projects, are focused vertically. Within the Technologies business sector, this includes Retail, Financial Services, Computer Management Services and Outsourcing. The function of Technology Projects is stated as being '... to provide technology-based methodologies which can be used by the verticals.' Although ideas for services are 'passed on to the verticals,' Technology Projects themselves have a channel to market through various other businesses they have grown. These include:

- multimedia development
- smart cards
- intelligence engineering
- performance engineering
- internet.

For example, the Internet business not only designs the pages, but also provides and manages the service. Colossus Computing currently manages the Internet pages for two major magazines. As Technology Projects is concerned with the generation and development of new ideas, the operations manager has two important roles. The first relates to technology strategy for Technology Projects and beyond to the whole of Colossus Computing. The second is concerned with responsibilities within the Operations division.

Within Colossus Computing, there is a Technology Strategy Board which has the role of setting policy and 'pulling together' different views on technology from different divisions and subdivisions of the company. The Technology Strategy Board is concerned mainly with the physical realization of technological ideas, and therefore is hardware-based. The operations manager of Technology Projects reports to the board regarding the adoption of technologies. An example is the case of smart cards, an area that was being looked at independently by Retail, Financial Services, and Technology Projects. Intervention by the Technology Strategy Board led to a commonality of views (and hardware) across different divisions.

Technology Projects' main purpose is the development of new ideas; the second role of the operations manager is a responsibility for the Operations division, which includes:

- skills transfer
- growing business.

To achieve this, attempts are made to identify future technology requirements, opportunities, and business areas through a 'technology watch'. This is facilitated through the development of 'future scenarios'.

FRONT-END PROCESSES

The following description of front-end processes at Colossus Technology Projects results from a series of interviews with Colossus Computing personnel. The definitions and diagrams have been developed as a result of the data collected.

Idea Development

The approach to product development taken in Colossus Technology projects is a fairly relaxed one. The term 'relaxed' is not used to suggest that it is taken lightly, or that it is performed badly – the track record of recent ideas appears very impressive. Rather, the actual genesis of an idea is a very complex process that is not understood easily and cannot be controlled completely. Different ideas are born in different ways, and too much structure at this creative stage may actually kill the goose that lays the golden egg. The fact that a large proportion of ideas will not be suitable for development for one reason or other would possibly be perceived as inefficient by some organizations. Colossus Computing, however, regard this phase as critical when compared to the expense of developing an unsuitable idea, or the profits achievable from a single good idea. Colossus Computing's understanding of the four phases of the lifecycle of new ideas/products was detailed by the operations manager, as well as the status of some current projects (Figure 5.2).

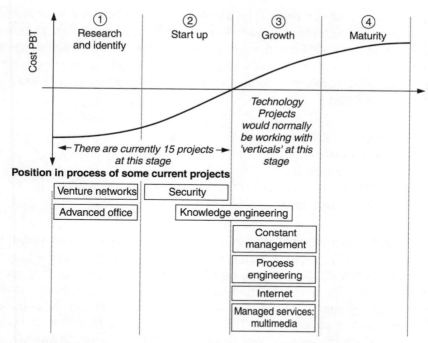

Figure 5.2 The four phases of the lifecycle of new ideas

Research and Identify

This phase can be separated into two separate stages:

1. cogitate and contemplate
2. dabble.

Cogitate and Contemplate

This stage involves loose, fairly unstructured research – what was described as 'getting a feel for what's going on.' It can involve consulting many information sources, including visiting customers, contacting academia, reading and so on. Any ideas generated are disseminated throughout the division by means of a bulletin that is produced every two to three months. This allows ideas to be exchanged and validated amongst Technology Projects personnel.

Ideas are screened regularly, usually every month. A single-sheet description of each idea is given to the meeting, and the descriptions are screened in an informal way by a core team. Decisions are made based on factors that include experience and gut feeling of team members. The screening team is usually fairly small at this stage, but would include:

- the technical director
- the operations manager
- a finance individual
- a marketing individual
- a personnel individual.

Only about 10 per cent of these ideas are normally 'perceived suitable for Enterprise Technology', and these will be allocated funding and progressed further. Depending on the nature of the idea, further idea development may be performed by one of the business units within Technology Projects. Ideas that do not pass are dropped, and no attempt is made to log them. The rationale for this is that with such a high turnover of ideas (90 per cent failure at this stage), 'if any of the ideas are important, then they will come up again anyway.'

It is noteworthy that the capability profile of Colossus Technology Projects is not a factor in the screening of ideas for development. It was explained that if a competency or capability that is not present within Colossus Computing is identified as necessary for the development of an idea, then it will be developed within Colossus Technology Projects. This aspect of competency and capability development is an important reason why a representative from personnel is involved in the screening process.

Dabble

At this stage, money begins to be spent on firming up the idea into a business proposal. Activities here may be performed by a team or just one person, taking typically between one week and two months, but never more than six months. It is here that the market is studied, usually for the first time, as ideas are often new-to-the-world developments or the result of technological development.

The output of the dabble stage is two- or three-page business case, which will include:

- concept description
- business value model (an examination of the market)
- distinctive capability model.

The failure rate at this stage is 80 per cent with only, 20 per cent of business cases being passed on to the start-up phase.

Start Up

During this phase, the concept is developed further with between £50 000 and £500 000 being allocated for this period. The outcome is a more detailed business case of approximately 10 pages.

Growth

A concept that makes it to this stage is normally passed to one of Technology Project's five businesses 'to be grown', and marketing begin to examine it formally. It is also usual for one or more of the verticals (i.e. those businesses within Colossus Operations that have a direct route to the market) to be involved with this phase. The business is grown and at the end of this phase the decision is taken whether to transfer the developed business to one of the verticals. It is not the role of Technology Projects to manage such developed concepts, explains General Manager B: 'Enterprise Technology don't own products, we own knowledge.'

Thus, most developed businesses are transferred to one of the verticals. If, for some exceptional reason, a business was not transferred, it would be added to those within Technology Projects.

FRONT-END PROCESS MODEL

From the above description, and from information given in interviews, a process model for the front-end activities at Colossus Technology Projects was formulated. This front-end process model is shown in Figure 5.3.

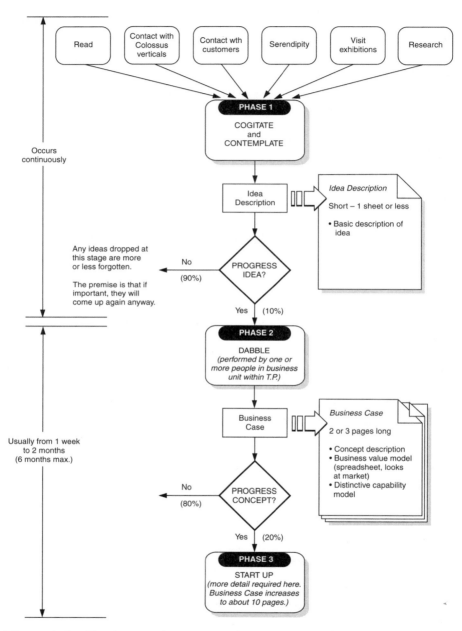

Figure 5.3　The front-end process at Colossus Technology Projects

Success

The success of Technology Projects is measured in two main ways: externally (the amount of revenue generated by verticals using new technology 'pulled through' or transferred from Technology Projects), and internally (the number of businesses grown by Technology Projects for transfer to verticals).

Skills and Competencies at the Front End

It was suggested that different skills and competencies are required during the various stages of the front-end process. In Phase 1 (cogitate and contemplate), the ideal person would:

- be a divergent thinker;
- be inquisitive;
- be a lateral thinker;
- possess good judgement; and
- have the ability to seek out relevant information.

For Phase 2 (dabble), the ideal person would be:

- a convergent thinker (from the abstract to the concrete); and
- able to firm up an idea.

The skills and capabilities of individuals within Technology Projects are utilized during product/service development. Personnel identify the specific skills of individuals, which then enables them to organize and locate skill as they are needed.

Consultancy Work

Technology Projects also provides consultancy to the verticals, and conducts workshops regarding process engineering and the process methodology that it has developed. Currently, such consultancy work for other divisions within Colossus Computing is unpaid, but it was indicated that this was under review, and may well change in the near future.

SPECIFIC APPROACHES TO REQUIREMENTS CAPTURE AND BUSINESS DEVELOPMENT

Interviews were conducted with key individuals responsible for product development within both the Technology Projects subdivision and its parent Colossus Operations division. The nature of the Colossus Computing investigations was different to those in the telecommunications and automotive companies. There was less access to personnel (four interviews in total) and, unlike in the other two companies, this access was not project-specific.

The research team conducted interviews with the following individuals:

1. The operations manager of technology projects, whose responsibilities include:
   - the generation of ideas for development; and
   - the management of the development process for Technology Projects and its businesses.
2. A systems architect involved in developing the business processes used by Colossus Computing.
3. The general manager of Multimedia Development, a business within Technology Projects, whose responsibilities include:
   - the development and management of the Multimedia Development business; and
   - the development of specific multimedia business solutions for client organizations.
4. The general manager of Managed Solutions, a business within Technology Projects, whose responsibilities include:
   - the development and management of the Managed Solutions business; and
   - the development of specific business service solutions for client organizations.

At least three members of the research team were present at all of the interviews. The interviews were semistructured, qualitative and covered four main areas:

1. The background of the interviewee.
2. The development of their respective business.

3. Their involvement in product development.
4. The activities that were undertaken at the front end of the development process.

The interviews were recorded on audio tape, the tapes transcribed and copies of the transcripts sent to the interview subjects for comment. The remaining part of this chapter summarizes the interview analysis and provides an insight into the individual approaches in the operations divisions to RC and business development.

MANAGED SOLUTIONS: GENERAL MANAGER B

GMB is the general manager of another business that was developed within Technology Projects, Managed Services. Due to its success, Managed Solutions was spun off from Technology Projects, and is now part of the autonomous businesses section of the operations division.

GMB's background has very much moulded his approach to the business. Approximately ten years ago, GMB was involved in a manufacturing operation within Colossus Computing in a customer service role. From there, he moved away from IT to become general manager of Colossus' Print Services operation for about three years. GMB returned to IT, which he considers his area of specialism, about eight years ago. In this time, he has developed a very process-orientated approach: 'I've really been managing through processes, rather than through technology.'

This approach has influenced the way in which solutions for customers' problems have been formulated: 'rather than come up with . . . a specific requirement and then go and seek a technical solution, I tend to build a solution around a process model and then go and find the products which actually suit my process model, rather than suit the requirements.'

This method of working stems from GMB's experiences five years ago, developing a customer service unit that delivered the internal IT requirements for Colossus. What began as a small help desk developed into a service centre, with total responsibility and accountability for IT delivery within Colossus Computing – employing 35 people and operating 24 hours a day, seven days a week. The development of this service was achieved by taking a process-orientated approach: 'What we built was this process model which we called FPMS – Formal Process Managed Solution. It was really just about formalization of the processes . . . we were then able to prove the processes and prove the interface . . . You then, obviously, have the basis of a very strong requirements spec. for a product.'

Once developed, this IT service was able to grow through the adoption of technologies rather than through a large increase in the number of staff. As GMB explains, 'Rather than bring more people in, where we actually found the technology, we brought the technology in which generated the capacity. And the capacity we generated, we then looked for something else to use it for.'

The service centre ended up managing approximately 120 mainframe applications across 80 sites in the UK, as well as another 80 worldwide.

Rather than using existing process modelling tools, which GMB believes produce, 'so much data that you really . . . suffocate yourself, and you can't move forward,' his approach is to sit down with a piece of A4 paper and start making 'a few scribbles'. This is much less formal, and based more on what he feels about the processes taking place: 'What you tend to find is that if you use the process model [tool], then I think you end up with too much detail to begin with. And if you start with a blank piece of paper, then the thing evolves around you . . .

MULTIMEDIA DEVELOPMENT: GENERAL MANAGER A

GMA is the general manager of Multimedia Development, a business developed and grown within Technology Projects, which is now an autonomous business developing multimedia solutions for client organisations.

GMA highlighted the importance of Colossus Computing's shift in business focus from hardware to software and services: 'In the 1960s it was 99 per cent hardware – software and services you gave away free . . . When you were selling a £5 million mainframe you could carry 50 or 60 people on the back of it, so you gave all that away free. Nowadays, that power you can deliver on a PC – you can't afford to give anything away free, you have to charge for the software and services. Now Colossus' revenues are probably 20 to 30 per cent hardware, 20 to 30 per cent software and more than 50 per cent is actually services.'

It is this shift that has necessitated Colossus becoming what GMA calls a 'people business', while the hardware side of the business – the 'non-people side' – has been reduced. 'We've been floating it [hardware business] off outside the company, or passing it across to Sanjumi, because they are still a big hardware manufacturer.'

GMA emphasized Technology Project's fundamental role within the operations division as a source of new technologies and methodologies: 'A people business needs "-ologies" – it needs technologies. It needs some part of the company to focus on what's coming next and to be the core centre of excellence, so that then can be rolled out across the company . . . and the company can learn from it. So, it's turning into a people business – changing the culture. Methodologies are one thing, somewhere in the company you need a focus on the other "-ologies"; the leading tech; the multimedia; computer telephony integration; data warehousing; the latest Internet/intranet; all the latest buzz words. Some part of the company has to focus on bringing those to market profitably.'

GMA defined his own role as follows: 'I pick up a newer "-ology", show how I can make it profitable; train up my staff; go and sell a few of them; develop the business; and then, potentially, hand it across to another part of Colossus to roll out.'

If a developed business becomes large enough, or successful enough it may be spun out of Technology Projects to become another autonomous business within Colossus Computing. However, it was pointed out that it would be more likely that a specific large project would be spun out, rather than the complete *business*: 'If you spun [the business] off, then Colossus wouldn't benefit from the reactive work that they're doing.

The principle, then, is to identify a potentially profitable technology prior to it being mass market, and to develop knowledge, skills and expertise in it so that when the technology takes off, Technology Projects are able to '. . . train up other parts of the company to take up tools, techniques, experience, and leverage it for the mass market.'

These technologies and methodologies are supplied as often to the other divisions within Colossus Technologies sector (Retail and Financial Services) as they are to the operations division. Most often, customers are not dealt with directly by Technology Projects businesses: 'We're there to help the organization sell to the customers.' Sometimes, however, potential customers are not considered worth dealing with by divisions such as Retail, for example, because they are too small: 'Those sort of people I deal with direct, because Retail are really dealing with the top...retailers. They've not bothered with [the small ones], so I handle it direct. But with others like Argos, Daewoo and Woolworths then I deliver...*through* Retail – so I am a component of their solution.

GMA's Multimedia Development business is always ahead of the verticals within Colossus Computing in the introduction of new technologies, despite often working in the same areas: 'Because it's leading-edge technology and I'm the leading part, so they're not in advance of me on any of my "ologies", like kiosk and Internet, I'm always leading them. And I know what they're doing because they're doing it with us.'

Although there is a Technology Watch Group within Technology Projects, each business still carries out its own activities. Multimedia Development undertakes both market-watch and technology-watch activities so that, as GMA states: 'We know what's going on in our market and we know what the clamour is from the account manager.'

It is recognized that, even though money can be made from reactive work – what GMA calls 'bread and butter' – doing proactive work and developing new technologies, services and solutions is vital: 'The bread and butter...would dry up if you're not gaining new skills. You've got to take the initiative and come up with a solution where you apply Java before somebody comes to you with a Java contract...You've got to apply the technology, so you've got to take a bit of risk in an area that's potentially going to give you your money back...'

The 'bread and butter' work is that done in order to leverage work for other parts of Colossus Computing. The value of this is approximately ten to one, i.e. Colossus Computing takes in revenue ten times what Multimedia Development deliver.

Route to Market

GMA's past experience made him aware of the importance of a clear route to market. About five years ago, GMA managed a CD-ROM and hypertext business within Colossus Computing called Imaging Solutions. Worth approximately £1 million, the intention of Imaging Solutions was to deliver both software and services, while owning the developed products. GMA encountered problems in reaching the market: 'I found that I didn't have my own sales channel and I was reliant upon the 500 salespeople in Colossus to sell my products. Now, they've already got a suitcase full of products and [although] mine might have been the best image products . . . they didn't understand them . . .'

The fact that the products were not understood fully by the salespeople, or that the salespeople understood other products better, meant that the Imaging Solutions products tended not to be 'taken out of their kit bag'. In addition, the salespeople tended to be reactive rather than proactive, and so they would wait for the customer to request a specific product rather than offer it as a potential solution.

This led to the realization that 'having the best product is not good enough,' and the formulation of specific objectives by GMA during the development of the multimedia business: 'I was determined this time that I was going to have my own specialist sales force that would either go direct to customers or go with the account managers to customers. So that the opportunity I knew was out there, I could actually reach. Whereas with Imaging [Solutions], I got this great product, and I put it on the shelf . . . and nothing happened. It was frustrating, I knew there were customers out there but I just couldn't reach them . . . I was determined this time to make sure I got the reach.'

Technology Projects' Integration Businesses

There are two main integration businesses within Enterprise Technology:

1. Multimedia Solutions
2. The Solution Centre.

While Multimedia Solutions has a multimedia focus, the Solution Centre is systems-integration focused, specializing in the integration of different manufacturers' computer hardware and software. Multimedia Solutions operates by doing consultancy work to create a multimedia solution for a customer, and then attempts to manage it for them: 'I want to get in the door, convince the customer that I've got a multimedia solution for him. I then want to do a systems integration job delivering it, and if I can I want to stay and get my foot in the door and say, "Well, rather than you manage it, how about I manage it?" and then I get rent roll.'

The Internet Business

Previous to starting Multimedia Development, GMA was involved in a CD-ROM and hypertext business worth approximately £1 million. Multimedia Development evolved from GMA's experience with Imaging Solutions and his belief that the Internet was commercially viable: 'I said, "I reckon this Internet is going to take off and there's lots of money to be made," and there was nobody doing anything in Colossus on the Internet, so it was an act of faith.

GMA's belief was based on experience and an understanding of the trends: 'It was gut feeling it was going to happen. Plus the trends were there, the fact that . . . if there's these thousands of people writing code for something, it will happen. These big organizations aren't just going to be able to stand up against it . . . I just saw it coming and said, "Let's jump on that bandwagon rather than set up our own network." '

Noticeably, GMA was given the go ahead to develop the Internet business *before* he had any customers for the service. In his mind, the technology was 'a goer' and he just had to find a way of getting into the market. This confidence on GMA's part was enough for his superiors to OK this development, indicating a fair degree of trust in GMA's competency in this area. GMA was given the go ahead by Technology Projects management and 12 months to show a profit. 'I was starting at the beginning of the year, so I'd got 12 months to solve it – because our budgetary cycle is 12 months . . . So I had to lose money for the first six months and then make it in the next six months as I got into the market.'

GMA's aim was to turn a £1 million business in CD-ROM and hypertext into a £3-million business in Internet: 'I took the CD-ROM hypertext business, used the skills to build an Internet business and I had a year to train myself, build a network and then start delivering profits to recover.'

The first work for the Internet business was acquired almost by chance. A salesperson from another business within Colossus Computing had approached a major book and magazine publisher. The publisher eventually told the salesperson that they were not interested in what was on offer, but just happened to mention another area of interest: 'The salesman was just closing the door and the guy says, "If you could just do me a little website, I'd be interested." ... We got the lead, [the salesman] was saying, "I don't know if it's worth anything but this guy maybe wants a website." We got in the door and then it mushroomed from that. So it was a throwaway comment from the customer.'

This one-liner fed back by the salesperson turned into a multi-million-pound opportunity for Multimedia Development. And this is often the case: 'A lot of them are like that, they're throw away comments that lead to an opportunity in the door.'

The publishing sector was where GMA and his small team were looking to identify an opportunity to use a website. By partnering the publisher, they were able to build them a website for the right market (one that would generate revenue for them) at a reduced cost. A website was built for a specific magazine produced by the publisher. This site had a forum for discussion and a job-searching facility, and was considered a great success by both partners in the project. 'We really built a community on the web and when we went live. People from 83 countries all around the world started looking there and there were 500 000 accesses a week. So it was a phenomenal success, a bigger success than they could have imagined.'

As advertisements would go not only in the published edition but also on the Web, there was an increase in the number of people wanting to place ads in the magazine. More jobs were being offered, and there was an increase in the number of people buying the physical journal. According to GMA, the publisher saw a very fast return on their investment: 'I think they reckon they recovered their money in 15 minutes.'

Since this success, Multimedia Development have been focusing on opportunities that will make money not just for them and Colossus Computing but also for the customer – encouraging others to jump on the bandwagon.

As the Internet business has become successful, so it has grown. In January 1995, there were 15 full-time personnel involved with the Internet business. By August 1996, that had increased to 150 – and they are currently taking on five people a week. The Internet business is made up of five separate teams:

1.   access team
2.   design team
3.   application development team
4.   managed service team
5.   integration team.

This is because for every part of a solution, a customer may need access to the Internet, some design work, some application work, ongoing managed service, and a way to actually integrate their own computer systems.

Electronic Shopping Mall

A recent development by Multimedia Development in the Internet industry is the electronic shopping mall. This concept came from the identification that individuals in countries far from the UK were very interested in 'Englishness' and buying 'English' goods. However, to obtain such goods, individuals were having to use specialist retailers who charged highly inflated prices.

Targeted at Japan and America, the aim was to offer high-value items and use the technology of the Internet, which was already being used in many of these countries, to sell them. It was decided that an Internet shopping site would be launched. Rather than selling local goods, which was being done by others, the idea was to sell high-brand 'English' goods at UK prices plus a delivery charge, with Multimedia Development getting a percentage of all transactions: 'There's a market there that wants it, we've got the medium now to get it to them, so why don't we address that? We believe there's a bigger market there for high-brand goods, certainly British goods and perhaps then, eventually, European goods, into America and Japan... rich societies with a lot of affluent people that like English products: let's get it to them.'

It was recognized that, in order to get people to visit the shopping site, it would have to offer more than just products for sale. As GMA explains: 'The concept of people just going to a shop means that they're only going to go there when they want something. We're making it an "interest" site. It's got details about Wimbledon and Henley – so anybody that wants to know about England comes to this site.'

The hope is that, while the browser is visiting the site, they will decide to buy something. This idea came from a brainstorming session that aimed to identify what was needed to get people to visit the site. The realization emerged that if the site contained merely products that were unlikely to change too often, then people would not keep coming back. However, if there were articles of interest, events and so on, then they would return. The electronic shopping mall had not been launched at the time of this study.

Kiosks Business

The kiosk business, like the Internet, sprang out of GMA's involvement with the CD-ROM hypertext business. A kiosk is a stand-alone unit that can offer CD-ROM multimedia facilities and allow different types of information to be accessed. Though originally loss-making, GMA was able to develop kiosk into a successful business within Multimedia Development: 'I took what was the beginning of a kiosk business (it was three people and two customers) that was making half a million pound losses, and I took that on at the beginning of the year... last year, I went from less than £1 million to a £3-million business and turned a new business in the Internet and a loss-making business in the kiosks to be... a million-pound profit.'

Businesses such as kiosk are a good example of the way leverage can be gained for other businesses within Colossus Computing. Sales of many other Colossus products and services may be obtained when GMA's kiosk business find a customer. 'If I do a job on kiosk then the company gets PC sales, software sales, consultancy sales, project management. So typically I leverage a factor of ten for the company more then I actually charge.'

By building a key capability in kiosks, Multimedia Development has become very competitive when tendering for any kiosk bid: 'Say Woolworths, or Daewoo, or Argos, or WHSmith want a kiosk solution – I can put my people in there and show we can come up with the best. We can come up with the best designs, the best price, the best delivery profile.'

As well as this reactive work, however, Multimedia Development attempts a more proactive approach to the kiosk market. This is based on GMA's entrepreneurial vision of the future of the kiosk market: 'I believe there's a big kiosk market coming: it's called the venture networks – and we're going to see them on every street corner ... The high ground would be to actually get in there early, open the kiosks and rent space out on them.'

To this end, Multimedia Development has launched very recently a kiosk for booking tickets for shows. It will automate the way in which the public buys tickets for plays, operas, concerts and other entertainment events. This idea was the result of what GMA calls 'a think tank' – a brainstorming session. The individuals that took part in this activity included all those involved with the kiosk business, the marketing person and GMA. They considered the question: 'How do we get ahead? What can you use kiosks for?'

The idea for a ticketing kiosk came out of this activity, and the decision was made to pre-empt the market, and develop the concept themselves: 'Rather than waiting for somebody to knock on our door, or perhaps somebody else to get there before us. Somebody's going to set up a kiosk network for ticketing, so why don't we do it?'

Multimedia Development collaborated with a box office ticketing company on the kiosk project. This company had a database already set up for booking tickets, and allowed Multimedia Development to use their name to market the kiosk concept to ticking agencies. The kiosk was linked to the collaborator's system, tickets were sold through them, and they were given 10 per cent commission.

Gut Feeling and Trust

The way in which GMA developed the Internet and kiosk businesses within Multimedia Development appears to indicate that a certain amount of gut feeling and trust is an accepted part of developing new products and business within Colossus Technology Projects. In the case of the kiosk business, GMA was given the go ahead for development by the managing director of Technology Projects on the strength of GMA's belief that it was a viable opportunity: 'Basically I said to [the Managing Director], "I reckon I can bring in £3 million by the end of the year ... so, Internet – I'm going to set up; the kiosk business – I'm going to turn round." And he says, "Well, all right then. Just don't cost me anything." He basically let me get on with it and I then went out looking for opportunities.'

The trust shown by the managing director of Technology Projects in GMA is based on the MD's understanding of GMA's past experience, capabilities and a belief in his business acumen. As GMA points out, 'It's trust and it's intuition. And it's a track record that builds the latter.'

Reactive and Proactive Projects

Businesses within Technology Projects are involved with two types of projects: reactive projects (project for people for money) and proactive projects (speculative and risk-taking projects).

In Multimedia Development, GMA likes to collaborate with other organizations to share the risk on proactive, speculative projects. For example, the Internet shopping mall idea was developed and refined in collaboration with a catalogue shopping company. This allowed the total cost (and risk) of developing a shopping site to be shared, while Multimedia Development gained experience in the area.

The more recent Internet shopping mall for 'English' goods was developed in a similar way. Multimedia Development collaborated with a high-street bank on its development, as a bank was needed to deal with the monetary transactions involved. '[The bank] were willing to ... put some money into some research ... I said, "We'll collaborate on this: we'll put in half a million ourselves. We'll put up the shopping mall and we'll see how it goes." And they're in it for the research side, we're in it for building a business.'

Wherever possible, Multimedia Development attempt to work with other businesses, that have finance and credibility, so that the collaborative venture there may create a new market opportunity.

SUMMARY

This case study reveals a number of contributory factors to success in new business development and RC:

- Emphasis on personnel and the right skills and competances for creativity.
- Providing the right environment, limited (controlled) structure, fast reactions, assessing all ideas, continual market and technology watch.
- Changing strategies to accommodate opportunities.

6

VANTAGE CASE STUDY

THE COMPANY

The Vantage Motor Vehicle Company is a major vehicle supplier producing one million vechicles per annum, globally.

Product Development at Vantage

Milestone Phases

Vantage has a development process known as the Project Management Policy (PMP). This procedure details eight phases and milestones for the product development as indicated in Figure 6.1. According to the product planning manager of Project C: 'Vantage has a process which is controlled through the PMP bible, so that from the earliest concept stage to production you go through phases and achieve a checklist criteria.'

The business planning manager of Project C explains the objectives behind milestones: 'Unless, and until, you meet certain objectives, you do not move forward... the project team... will be reporting up higher in the business. As part of the philosophy here, we have milestone events where we do that. There are also formal reports that will go to the board.'

Checklist criteria at milestones are imposed to weed out bad ideas. The criteria may involve activities that range from undertaking detailed customer information, competitor information, industry

Predevelopment → Design Zero → Design Zero Two → Design One →
Quality Maturation → Manufacturing Phase → Volume Phase → Post Launch Phase

Figure 6.1 The stages of Vantage's project management policy

intelligence, legal and safety issues, appearance, performance, ergonomics and standards. This is to ensure the development of the programme is undertaken in an efficient manner and run to time schedules. These milestones indicate to teams when certain tasks should be completed. If it is felt the team has not completed the criteria set to the project, then the programme will not be allowed to continue to the next phase.

For example, a brand manager explained that their task is to complete various commercial activities at each stage of the PMP, which becomes gradually more detailed as the project progresses: 'At phase D0 [Design zero], a list of activities have to be done such as some market research, a price proposal and volume assumption.'

The PMP acts as a set of guidelines or policy for delivering projects. The business planning manager for Project C explained the purpose of the PMP: 'It is not rocket science; it divides up a programme into a number of milestone phases . . . gateways. Vantage divides them into chunks enabling us to develop and monitor programmes . . . Giving confidence in what we are doing . . . we will deliver a profitable, professional-quality product into the market at the right time.'

Although all projects have individual differences, problems and similarities, the following case study represents a typical overall view of the development process that may be carried out in Vantage and the relationships within this.

Stage 1: Predevelopment Phase

The activities involved in predevelopment are shown in Figure 6.2.

Concept Generation

> *The background to any programme starts off with requirements one way or another. That goes back to the corporate plan of the organization.*
>
> Business planning manager, Project C

A vehicle idea may be developed through either a market sector requirement or a new market requirement that is linked to the corporate plan. The corporate plan covers a five-year horizon, but is

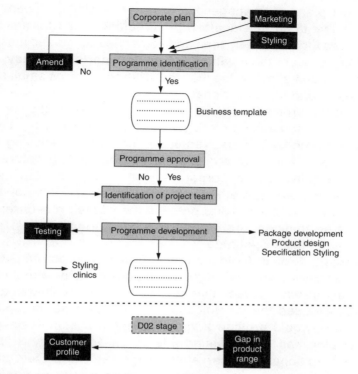

Figure 6.2 The predevelopment phase

reviewed on a yearly basis to take account of possible market or customer requirements that the company has not addressed or feels the market is ready to take on board. As the project director of Project A explains: 'Every year the organization reviews its corporate plan and looks at market trends worldwide and sees sectors we feel we need to operate in. From time to time, we identify a sector where the organization is not currently represented and we feel we should fill that sector.'

Corporate planning will map out a broad indication of the proposition, e.g. the market sector it will enter, the scope and size of engine and the rough physical size of the project (or the 'package'). Once a requirement has been identified, 'you will get a buy in from the business to say this is what we need to be in by this time frame' (business planning manager, Project C).

A product planning manager for Project B explains, 'There is no bold route identified that deals with screening ideas formally; it is creative. If an idea has been seen and someone recognized the potential, a small concept team will be set up to undertake a study, given two to three months to develop the idea. This could be as small as four to five people and multifunctional . . .'

However, requirements are not just identified through the corporate plan, as a product planning manager for Project B explains: 'Vantage has lots of off-the-wall ideas. Vantage is not good at sticking to our corporate plan as a lot of projects derive from styling before there has been a need in the corporate plan, then the plan catches up . . . Processes are something all companies are developing. At the end of the day it is hard to process the whole procedure; much relies on free thinking and ideas and brainstorming ideas, people taking on a pet like or pet hate.'

For example, Project A did not derive from the corporate plan. The concept was developed from a gut feeling of a director who identified strategic and product issues that needed to be addressed in a given area. This included the identification that broadening the appeal of Vantage cars would provide a wider potential customer base. The corporate plan had not identified this as an opportunity to discard Vantage's traditionally conservative image. As the project director of Project A explained, 'the market and media refer to our buying public as between 55 and dead.' Secondly, a product issue was identified through a gap in the Vantage small-car strategy, between Vantage 100 and the old 200, as the project director of Project A commented: 'Vantage discovered a gap between Car A and Car B, not in the market place but in our range.'

Central marketing often initiate and trigger projects to be developed, as with the new medium-large car. Marketing were 'working on the project before the team was set up . . . looking at the large-car market to identify customer requirements . . . the research dovetailed straight into the project team,' (brand manager, Project B).

Market research is conducted with the aim of producing vehicle concepts through, for example, findingt 'more innovative ways to look at the market and understand what people want, to give us products that would be different from competitors,' (brand manager, Project B).

A typical marketing project may try to discover for example, what customers want their vehicle to do, or what customers need from a vehicle. Through this, customers can be grouped into clusters based on their needs, as opposed to traditional automotive segmentation, such as they drive a medium car so they are medium-car people.

Concept Initiation

Following basic concept approval, the programme is identified further on the basis of scale, finance and time to market.

The proposition from the corporate plan will be reviewed around the organization at high levels of management in the business, and discussed on an annual basis, amended and agreed by the main board. The board may then say 'we like that' or 'Go away, think again and come up with a different profile.'

If the programme requirements are agreed, then a business template is formed by the business planning staff who 'take the plan's assumptions and try to convert it into a business template concept [according to the] concept of the corporate plan (business planning manager, Project C).

At this point the programme is reviewed by the main board to examine relevance to market requirements, and the financial and human resource profile of the business. The direction of the product concept is decided. Here, the character of the vehicle may be approved in relation to the corporate plan. As a business planning manager for Project C suggests, 'The profile is screened at corporate level to see if the project is addressing the market requirements identified...the financial profile...and human resource profile of the business.'

If the programme is rejected at this point, then the programme will be reviewed and amended. If approved, the identification of a project team is established. Although this may be just 'a small group of people who look at a proposition and develop a proposal for the products positioning and features, the team would take the philosophy to start developing the concept to produce a programme. They will flesh out the basic design philosophy, define specification thinking about designing in detail, about the market...volumes...pricing... profitability...technologies, materials...' (product planning manager, Project B).

Product Design Specification

The programme is developed further, by testing the concept against given criteria. This may involve research, personal experience, other development programmes, and commercial and technical aspects. As a business planning manager (Project C) explains: 'There has been a broad profile at the corporate plan level ... but until you have more detailed work you will not know how realistic some initial estimates are.'

At this point, the product design specification is developed to ensure the philosophy of the product, the size, weight, cost, testing etc. is set out. Small renderings or coloured drawings may have been developed to identify design alternatives for the concept. Package drawings may be conducted to specify a wide range of parameters, e.g. leg room, boot space, suspension location, engine compartment.

The product template indicates all possible product configurations and styles to be considered at the milestone. For example, on Project A, the chief engineer and product planning manager explained how the possible style designs were generated: '... the shape came from styling; the company wanted something new and different. Styling got six young designers for two weeks, asked them to design something different, and had a competition day.'

Figure 6.2 depicts the main stages involved in Vantage's predevelopment phase, from the generation of concepts, to the initial firming of the general philosophy of the concept. Figures 6.3 and 6.4 demonstrate the conceptualization of two of the projects (Projects A and B) investigated in the research.

Stage 2: Design Zero Phase

Following configuration and style possibilities considered at the end of the predevelopment phase, product selection will be undertaken. This selection may be taken through a formal internal programme review. The programme will then be further developed in the detailed programme development stage, where the project will pass to programme approval. As a business planning manager (Project C) explains: 'At that stage, we are picking up the agreed product selec-

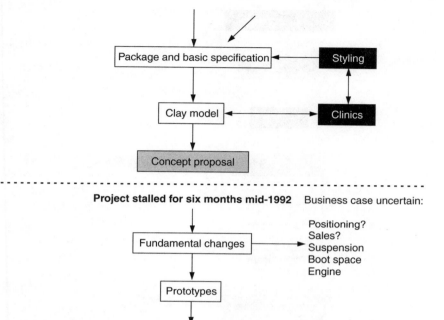

Figure 6.3 Conceptualization of Project A

tion and coming up with a detailed programme to deliver this vehicle to an agreed costed programme and time frame.'

At this stage of selection, internal review and approval allows projects to be screened thoroughly to reject any that may need redefining. As the business planning manager for Project C suggests, 'This is part and parcel of project development; not all projects will run. If the investigation shows you have not got it right, for example, if [the project] cannot deliver 0 to 130 miles an hour in five seconds, and that is perceived to be important, then there is no point pursuing the programme.'

This process allows development projects to be stalled to avoid unnecessary spending of resources. As the chief engineer and pro-

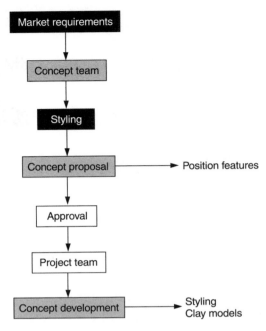

Figure 6.4 Conceptualization of Project B

duct planning manager explained, Project A was initially stalled for six months: 'The concept proposal went forward for the car but the business case did not work well because the car was a bit expensive and positioning in the market was uncertain. The project was then stalled . . . some aspects did not meet what we wanted, for example, how much money it was going to make for us.'

Styling and seating bucks (clay models) may be refined through detailed drawings of the proposed shape and interior, leg room, control locations, trim etc. Also at this stage, the clay models will be shaped by hand or computer aided design (CAD) to form fibreglass models to enable further testing and development to continue. By the end of phase Design zero, a price and all the features will have been fixed. As the product planning manager for Project B explains, at this point it is a case of '. . . sealing the specification of the car and engineering so they know exactly what they have to deliver. At that point we have to control carefully the cost and the feature inclusion.' This phase may take up to two years, and is shown in Figure 6.5.

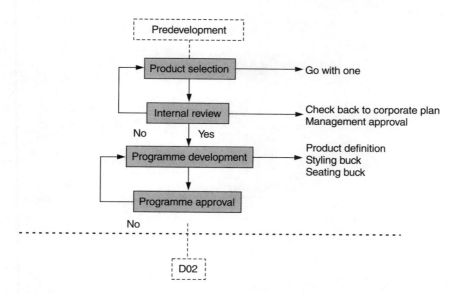

Figure 6.5 Design zero phase

Stage 3: Design Zero 2 Phase

The Design Zero 2 phase shown in Figure 6.6 concentrates on the development of engineering design to build an engineering design concept. Here, the manufacturing team become involved to allow the development of the manufacturing facility to begin. Areas of specialism (ASO) personnel will enter the development phase; these are '... groups of experts [separate from project teams] concentrating on technical areas like chassis, powertrain, electrical and trim etc...' (business planning manager, Project C).

Stage 4: Design 1 Phase

The Design 1 phase involves the validation of the engineering design to set out how the vehicle will actually be built, through testing the design. A prototype may be made as close to production as possible. This allows the team to develop a proven engineering design that they can support. At this stage, design information will be issued to manufacturing who undertake costing and tooling studies for assembly to

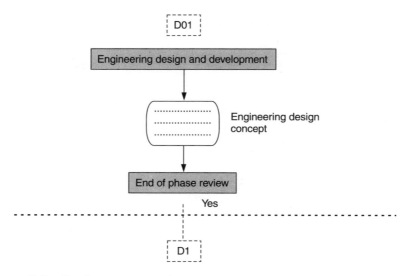

Figure 6.6   Design zero two phase

support the manufacturing facility. By the end of this phase all major components will be frozen and only minor adjustments will be feasible, as depicted in Figure 6.7.

Stage 5: Quality Maturation Phase

The quality maturation phase (Figure 6.8) enables the vehicle to be built in the right way to mature the quality and prove the supply chain. Vantage has a quality policy setting out ISO requirements. This may involve building steel prototypes of the vehicle, and testing (in the laboratory) the body shell and mechanical assemblies, e.g. noise, harshness, vibration and fatigue.

Stage 6: Manufacturing Phase

The manufacturing phase (Figure 6.9) enables the manufacturing facility to be validated, 'to bed down the manufacturing facility you have established earlier, probably in the D1 phase' (business planning manager, Project C), and to prove the quantity and quality of the vehicle. Machine installation and vehicle tests are also conducted. By

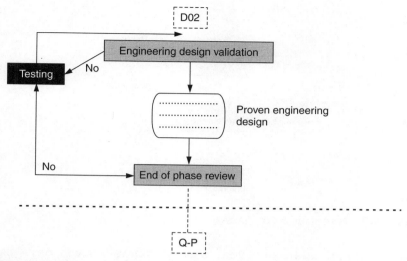

Figure 6.7 Design one phase

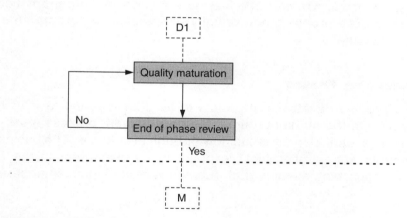

Figure 6.8 Quality maturation

the end of this phase, dealers and distributors will be educated and informed so as to attain their commitment to the project.

Stages 7 and 8: Volume and Postlaunch phases

These phases (Figure 6.10) validate the volumes to be manufactured following launch of the product. The launch programme will have

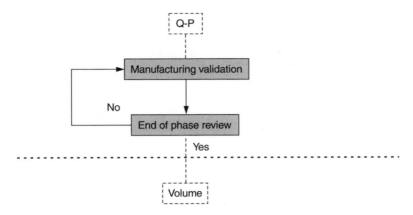

Figure 6.9   Manufacturing phase

started approximately one year earlier; marketing will have been involved to develop the communications plan through briefing advertising agencies, writing trade literature and developing promotional activities. The project team formally hands over the programme to manufacturing.

Overlapping Phases

For a product development project to be effective, and to launch a product into the market on time, the development process must not run in a sequential manner but flow through the phases. The business planning manager of project C explains that Vantage recognizes this: '... an important element [is] running simultaneous engineering,

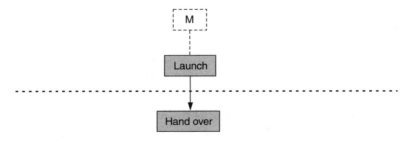

Figure 6.10   Volume and postlaunch phase

making sure things do not happen sequentially but can happen simultaneously, which brings risks but also brings great opportunities in the market perspective.'

Future Developments

It must be pointed out that because vehicles have lifecycles of approximately six to eight years, and the whole development process may take up to 12 years, although a vehicle may have just been launched, Vantage has concepts aiming to replace existing models and has ideas for vehicle improvements approximately one year before an existing vehicle is due to launch. This is due to the incremental nature of development, working on how a vehicle will be improved in two or three years as a half-life face lift. As the chief engineer and product planning manager from Project A explained, 'People started working on the car for the year 2000 last year, but it will only be going from 1997 when they say go for it.' Such work involves collecting information on problems that have arisen with the current model, carrying out packaging studies, making full-size models and testing the image for a Vantage in the year 2000.

PROJECT TEAMS FOR DEVELOPMENT PROJECTS

The management style behind project teams at Vantage aims at providing 'empowerment to a group of individuals who collectively have a range of skills that can take a concept idea and develop it into a proper vehicle programme for development' (business planning manager, Project C). At Vantage, the development teams are given a certain amount of leeway to carry out the PMP, although there must be strict adherence to the milestone phases.

Organization of Teams

Functional Competence

Teams are essentially guided by their project directors who have, 'a first-line team covering all the core competencies required' (business planning manager, Project C). All relevant players across the business are represented on a project team, including commercial, manufacturing, engineering, product planning, project management and finance personnel. A typical project may consist of a project director, a chief engineer, a brand manager, manufacturing engineers and design engineers. Teams may grow to over 300 people at any one time; even small teams such as Project A consist of up to 70 people. The team can at any time, bring in other people. For example, a project may have design engineers coming on board in their area of specialism, e.g. chassis, body, trim, to do the design work then the validation work. When this is completed, their contribution has been satisfied and they will move on somewhere else. Resources typically belong to the relevant central core resource and people are 'borrowed' for the duration of projects.

The chief engineer and product planning manager for Project A explains the benefit of the ability to draw resource from a central area: 'You keep refreshing people's knowledge, they go back, do advanced work in the core, and come out again on a project.'

The business planning manager for project C explains how, over the years, Vantage has become more sophisticated in the way they link together and build on mutual skills of the resources available: 'For example, the manufacturing engineer will be working alongside the design engineer to make sure the design the stylist chooses to run with is something that can be made well.'

Inter- and Intrapersonal Competence

Part of the PMP process is to identify teams. As the business planning manager for project C explained, 'The mechanism varies from team to team, but we try to use the Belbin technique to select a cross-section of people.'

Vantage has recognized the theoretical benefits of the Belbin technique: the project teams attempt to draw people with a variety of personalities and inter- and intra-personal competencies allowing an atmosphere that is 'mutually supportive rather than, for example, all visioneers. You need some visioneers, some chairpeople, some completer–finishers etc.' (business planning manager, Project C).

Areas of Specialism

Areas of specialism fundamentally own component parts of a vehicle, such as chassis, electrics, trim, hardware, body or safety equipment. These are brought into project teams but are expected to look to the future and co-ordinate trends they pick up from supplier and manufacturing capabilities.

Decision Making

A change in decision making had been carried out in the company. Previously, decisions were made on a hop-down basis, which could cause delays in product development, as the project director of Project A explains: 'If you have a hierarchical process, it makes decisions difficult; the consequence is no-one makes decisions and avoids it.' Now, all judgements on products are delegated to the product team and engineers. 'Our decisions were made locally; once we committed ourselves, we reported, saying this is what we have done.'

MARKETING AND THE PRODUCT DEVELOPMENT PROCESS

Marketing at Vantage has a critical role to play in the development of vehicles, from initiating ideas to launching the vehicle. Marketing is used constantly throughout the stages of a development programme. This section shows how marketing is organized for development projects and how it is exploited as a resource in the development of a vehicle.

The business planning manager for Project C explains: 'Previously, Vantage would engineer a programme because it seemed good to do. We are now looking at programmes that not only you can engineer, but you can make, sell profitably and address market requirements.' According to the chief engineer and product planning manager of Project A, [Marketing] forced us to change the concept.

Strategic Input

Marketing and the Corporate Plan

Vantage has a five-year company-wide plan, and marketing has its own version (as do all functions). Marketing plans are reviewed twice a year, rewritten at the end of every year, and completely revised every five years.

Marketing's strategic role in product development is viewed as a mechanism to portray the market and environment as it is today, and in the future for products to be launched into. Marketing, although a separate department, feed into the corporate plan at the front end, as a director of Project A explains: 'We have constant feedback from market research agencies and academia to look at the emergence of perceived issues and real issues.'

As the automotive market is so competitive, manufacturers are looking to ascertain strategic possibilities for future developments early on. These may look as far ahead as the year 2015, but are focused down to look five years ahead.

The project director of project A explained how marketing helps the corporate plan move forward by looking at softer issues involved in enhancing product value: 'What will a Vantage product vision look like in 2002? Looking at the product strategy, you start to feel what the product is like from marketing expressions and the need to change things tangibly to let engineers work with it . . . Expressions can reveal the difference between attributes and features, for example the difference between interior lighting (an attribute) and the light (a feature).'

Marketing Plans

Marketing plans are formulated at the beginning of development pro-grammes to detail key activities to be completed before launching the vehicle. The milestones laid down by the PMP indicate when detailed work has to be undertaken. At the beginning of a project, key events and actions are identified to be completed by each milestone. Actions to be taken for a full year ahead are identified and reviewed each quarter.

Launch Campaigns

When a vehicle is approaching the manufacturing phase, marketing will be involved tactically to develop a launch campaign through brief-ing advertising agencies, organizing the launch event and promo-tional material etc. However, the project team is involved in any decisions, via the brand manager, in order to penetrate all aspects of the new vehicle. As the business planning manager of Project C explains: 'We are interested in working as a project team because we do not want our car to be launched into nothing ... We have conversations with [advertising] agencies to discuss how to position it. It is important, particularly when you have an incremental programme, to make sure you position it or reposition the new model in an appropriate way not to undermine the position you already have.

Gathering Marketing Information

Marketing information is normally gathered through the central sales and marketing department of the Vantage Motor Vehicle Company, and disseminated to the project team through the brand manager. This enables, all members of the team to have access to the marketing data. This marketing information is diffused through relevant players involved in the programme, as the business planning manager for Project C comments: 'As you get closer to the marketplace, the information will be shared with our national sales companies, to the dealer organizations who are expected to validate the assumptions being made on their behalf effectively.'

The role of marketing at Vantage is summed up well by the brand manager of Project B: 'Vantage recognizes planning has to happen at the beginning. Sales and marketing input is valuable even before we have engineers on the project. When engineers come on board, there is more definition. The initial profile and outline of requirements have to be specified before there is any real development work on the car.'

The Structure and Organization of Marketing

Structure

The structure of marketing at Vantage is shown in Figure 6.11. Marketing is fundamentally based with Vantage Cars, who control brand management, marketing strategy and market research. LandVantage has a separate marketing department, but must go to Vantage Marketing to access resources such as market research. The brand managers based within project teams at both Vantage cars and LandVehicles report directly to the core brand management facility,

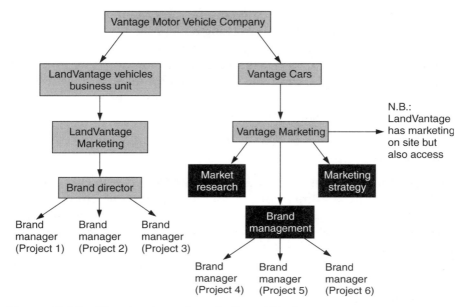

Figure 6.11   The structure of marketing at Vantage

which, in turn, may access marketing resources requested for development programmes.

The Organization of Marketing

Marketing is represented on project teams in the form of a brand manager designated from the central resource of the sales and marketing function. Brand managers are assigned to projects as the commercial representative. For example, brand managers each work on projects for a vehicle replacing Project A and on every vehicle project. Brand managers are responsible directly to marketing, because brand managers are part of that central resource but have a 'dotted line' responsibility to a project team.

The role of a brand manager on a project is 'to interface between the project team [or engineering business units] and markets selling the car; to talk to markets and understand what products they require; to interpret those requirements and feed those to the project team [or the engineering business unit],' (brand manager, Project B).

Another aspect of a brand manager's role is to interface with both the marketing strategy department and market research department, also based in the sales and marketing function. Marketing strategy is responsible for projecting how the future vehicle market will develop across the world. For example, as Project B's brand manager asks, 'What is the size of the car market for large cars, small cars, 4×4 in each different place?'

Brand managers also interface with the market research department, who are responsible for liaising with customers. Market research provides vital information to 'understanding what ongoing project they have, the changing marketplace, how people's requirements are changing and what customers think is important,' (brand manager, Project B).

Market Research

The brand manager for project B explains the importance of market research: 'The end user has got to have more input so it [the vehicle] is designed as the right product for the market.'

The process that a typical brand manager may conduct to research issues is depicted in Figure 6.12.

Market research in Vantage is used as a risk-reducing mechanism to eliminate further costs and resources later in the development process. As the brand manager for Project B explains, 'There was a recognition that Vantage has to do a lot of work up front, to have an understanding of what you want to do before you go out and do it [to avoid unexpected problems].' The chief engineer and product planning manager for Project A adds: 'When a car is launched, it is criticized in ways you never anticipated, so you may be panicking to do something to respond.'

Market Research is not an infallible tool; it is only as good as the people interpreting it. For example, disasters such as the Ford Edsel of the late 1950s where the result of failure of image studies to detect a shift in American car buyers' attitudes. Nevertheless, Vantage believes that if market research is conceived intelligently and interpreted cautiously, it has considerable power to identify unsuspected groups of potential buyers and gaps in the market.

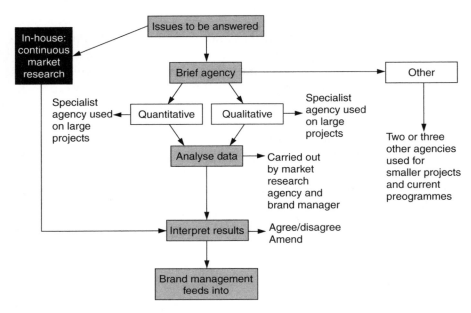

Figure 6.12   Market research process for a development project

Briefing Agencies

Prior to briefing agencies, the product development team (through the brand manager) are asked whether they require any specific issues to be raised in the research. As a brand manager explains: 'The team does research because we need answers to questions and not research everything we want answers to.'

Vantage recognizes that to get value out of agencies, and give them scope to interpret, the agencies have to understand how the research fits in. 'Experience over the years has showed whoever is doing the research must be well briefed,' (brand manager, Project B).

Vantage has attempted to do this by bringing agencies into their confidence and giving them as much information as possible: 'We explain our strategy and what we want to do to make sure they understand the strategic issues. Then the agency knows the issues to probe for, questions to ask, and have a good understanding of the car and how it fits into the bigger picture of the marque as a whole,' (brand manager, Project B).

Research Activities

Agencies are brought into Vantage development programmes as and when required; they may be brought in more than once throughout the development programme to focus on a number of different aspects. Agencies may be brought in approximately three years before the launch of the vehicle for three main reasons: to understand positioning, acceptability and styling (although separate styling clinics are carried out by internal design experts). The different tools and techniques used by both Vantage and another automotive company surveyed are shown in Table 6.1.

In the case of project B, agencies were used 12 months prior to the launch of the vehicle, to develop a detailed marketing platform for the vehicle to be launched on. This research is conducted to understand strengths, issues and positioning against other vehicles, who it appeals to and its target audience.

Building Relationships

Vantage has a number of agencies that brand managers can choose from, usually depending on the type of work required. Typically, Vantage uses one agency for qualitative work and one for quantitative, while there are a number of others that Vantage uses for smaller or current programmes. As the brand manager of Project B suggests, 'For vehicle development, Vantage uses a couple [of agencies] who are familiar with the long-term plans.' The use of a small number of agencies is for two reasons: because of the sensitive nature of the development projects undertaken, and to build a rapport with agencies they can trust, allowing Vantage to be open with information outside of development programmes.

Vantage also tries to utilize market research agencies in a more practical form, so that information that is gathered is not necessarily raw, e.g. 'Ten per cent of people said. . . ' This forces agencies to think through user comments and their implications, and to use their interpretation skills to formulate recommendations.

This information is then fed back to the project development team through the brand managers, and the team debates what action should be taken based on the findings.

Table 6.1   Definition and use of market research techniques

Technique	Description and use
JATO	This is a syndicated database that car manufacturers can access to allow comparison of competitor products by feature and model as the brand manager at company A explained: 'It will print out the differences and similarities between, for example, an xxx and xxx, down to, for instance, one has got a glove box and the other does not . . . it can do it against every car in the UK . . . and all of Europe.'
NCBS	The New Car Buyers Survey is a syndicated survey that all of the main car manufacturers provide funding for. This survey produces information regarding: why customers have purchased, the likes and dislikes of past and present vehicles owned, demographics etc. The NCBS has a response of over 30 000 customers a year.
Quality surveys	Quality surveys gather information regarding problems that have occurred under warranty. An agency may conduct a telephone survey between three and six months after the vehicle was purchased to talk through a questionnaire, to establish satisfaction ratings with the product and service received, and to evaluate whether the product has lived up to the expectations of quality and reliability.
Qualitative focus groups: issue groups/social trends	Up-to-date or emerging issues may be discussed in a focus group to ascertain respondents' views and concerns about such issues as environmental impacts of the car industry, safety issues etc. These help to assess how people may react to developments in the industry and steer new technology.
	Company A uses the Henley Planning for Social Change to look, in a general sense, at lifestyles and situations five to ten years in the future, and to assess how trends and demographics are going to change. This aims to understand how people in the market are going to be different in the future.

Technique	Description and use
Image surveys	Image surveys look at a company's perceived image in the market against competitors, to see strengths, weaknesses and what people think the company is good at.
Clinics: positioning, use of clay modelling	Clinics are used to investigate the complexities of vehicle, and the diversity of issues involved, such as aesthetics, ergonomics, dynamics and functionality. The protracted and sequential nature of a new vehicle development results in the situation where clinics can never address all the product attributes in a realistic combination until the vehicle is virtually complete and out of the development phase.
	Clinics may select a relevant sample and carry out competitive product testing. This will involve displaying the vehicles of the same fashion, colour and standard to remove bias.
	In concept development, three-dimensional clay models, full-size clay models, package clinics, glass, reinforced plastic/fibreglass and prototypes may be used in a clinic. At preproduction phase, vehicles may be presented in metal to test the final specifications. Techniques that may be used in clinics include self-completion questionnaires, interviews, mini groups and full-group discussion.
Tracking surveys	These are conducted on a continual basis to establish trends in the market/customers. For example, advertising tracking surveys are undertaken to establish how a new launch has been received by the market.
Early buyers feedback	Surveys are sent to new car buyers after three to six months to gather information on whether the vehicle is living up to expectations and feeding back information for future projects or facelifts.

Market Research Techniques used in Development Projects

Techniques used by a team or research department vary from stage to stage throughout the development process. Figure 6.13 shows the various research techniques that can be called upon for developing

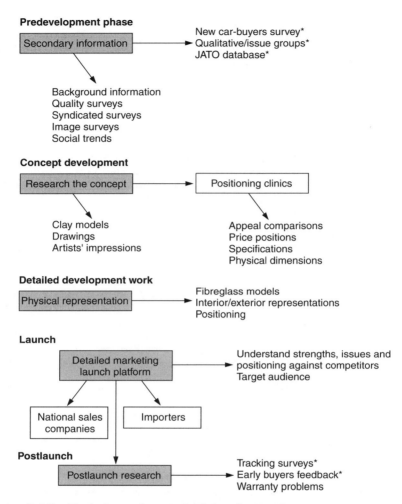

Figure 6.13   Techniques for product development

products. Those indicated by an asterisk (*) are described in Table 6.1.

Market and Design

The interrelationship between the design function and the brand manager at Vantage for development projects is close. Designers are given not only the physical dimensions of the vehicle in a brief (e.g. the engine size and body style) but also the soft factors (e.g. 'a car with character' or communication elements and image statements to allow design to build these factors into the vehicle). These soft factors have been generated from research undertaken at the beginning of a project, for example image-associated factors that may be important to a specific target market for a vehicle. Hence marketing is assisting design in a proactive manner, rather than being prescriptive, in an attempt to exceed customer expectations.

The designers are given a free reign to develop what they think meets the brief. The designers define what the vehicle needs and what they think is appropriate for the market. Design may then develop up to five sketched ideas. These may come from the internal design function or an external design agency. The design team give their recommendations based on their judgmental views. As the brand manager of Project B explains, 'Design do not have absolute say but they have the opportunity to influence products chosen.' However, the ultimate decision of which design to go with is very much team-based.

EXTERNAL RELATIONSHIPS AND PRODUCT DEVELOPMENT

Supplier Involvement

Once the major components have been identified, suppliers are chosen in tiers through the life of a project, as the product planning manager for Project B explains: 'The PMP has milestones where we have to have nominated so many [suppliers].' Prior to this, the supplier will have to have 'demonstrated they can meet our requirements, in terms of quality, cost, sharing information and databases.'

The sharing of information between Vantage and its suppliers is crucial in the development of any vehicle. For example, suppliers may develop new technologies to shape doors, handles and wings, which, in turn, may help the team to achieve a new design, where traditional manufacturing methods may not. Hence, the supplier can have a lot of influence in helping make decisions for product development.

Suppliers are essentially brought into the process up front to take knowledge from their suppliers early on. As soon as they are liaising with the team, supplier staff become part of that team to enable the team to draw on the best knowledge and specialist skills for a given component for a system. However, the business planning manager for Project C specified that most work with suppliers is concentrated into a number of stages, namely 'the design development, validation and manufacturing process.'

Dealer Relationships

Dealers are used as the first point of contact with the end user, and a company may test their opinions. However, no direct research is undertaken with dealers; their main role is still to sell and support the product in the marketplace. Dealers do not enter the development process until very late because they 'do not necessarily help you to design new products,' (business planning manager, Project C). However, dealers are brought into development through key dealer groups to 'show them the product 12 or 18 months before launch,' (brand manager, Project B). Again, however, Vantage does not particularly elicit their views. Nevertheless, dealers do play a key role in providing information. For example, sales figures, warranty returns, and their views on where they think Vantage is going in the future, which is fed back into the team.

Relationships with Distributors

Distributors' input into product development is indirect (similar to that of dealers). Events are undertaken every quarter to inform distributors of product updates, to provide product information and to allow them to have a chance to convey their views and comments vehicles in development.

SUMMARY

Product Development at Vantage

- The product development process at Vantage attempts essentially to take into consideration the first trappings of a project, and identifies this through the predevelopment phase. This predevelopment phase attempts to identify which projects should or should not be taken forward into further development phases.
- All ideas that are put forward follow the same process of being accepted, rejected or shelved.
- The front end is primarily driven by corporate planning and marketing.
- The strength of an idea can be increased if key personnel, such as senior executives, buy in to specific ideas.
- All projects contain teams who align to core functions and resources. This allows the core departments to be called upon for information, co-ordination, advice and resources when requested, to maximize the input any one resource may have.

Marketing/Market Research and Product Development

- Information capture at the front end concentrates on gathering marketing information to allow exploration of market trends, worldwide trends and customer attitudes towards new and existing products in the hope that this will generate either market or customer requirements.
- Vantage utilizes its marketing activities, such as market research to ensure the company does not destroy an existing customer base when developing new products, and invests in developments that will raise their appeal to a wider buying market.
- Market research is utilized throughout the development programme of a project to explore different concepts early on and to support or validate any assumptions that have been made in the later stages of a vehicle's development.
- The development of relationships with external market research agencies is crucial to the enhancement and acceptability of new products put into the market. Their input is brought in as an opportunity to liaise directly with the end user to answer specific

questions and issues that a project team may be unsure of regarding the market and users.

• Market research tools and techniques vary from the use of in-house surveys to gather information from warranty problems to techniques used by agencies such as focus groups to explore wider issues related to the industry as a whole. The different tools and techniques used are outlined in Table 6.1 and Figure 6.12.

• Marketing have an important role to play in feeding the design function information from the market. The information is translated to design in a form that they can use, with their imagination, to develop innovative vehicle concepts.

External Relations and Product Development

Although relationships with suppliers, dealers and distributors are close, it is only the suppliers who are bought into the development process to any extent. Dealers and distributors are involved once the basic product concept and requirements have been decided.

7 BANDAGE CASE STUDY

This chapter was written by Liz Barnes and Margaret Bruce.

INTRODUCTION

The woundcare market is a fairly traditional one, encompassing products that range from simple bandages to slightly more complex odour-control absorbent dressings. Few new-to-world products are launched in this market. New products tend to consist of product line extensions or improvements to existing products. Since RC has improved NPD processes in high-tech companies, this case study will address the use of RC in this more traditional market, in order to improve NPD and meet the demands of this dynamic market.

Trends in Medical Textiles

In the field of medical textiles, perhaps one of the most important areas to consider is the treatment of wounds, which is indeed one of Bandage's core therapy areas. Historically, this treatment was carried out in hospitals, but it is increasingly carried out by practice nurses, district nurses and community nurses, with over 71 per cent of patients receiving treatment in their own homes, an average of three times a week, accounting for 50 per cent of district nurses' time (Caring for the Community, Bandage Healthcare, 1994). Rainey (1995) said, 'Since the mid 1980s, there has been a growing interest in wound care and an enormous growth in new products.'

It is estimated that in the Western world, the prevalence of leg ulcers is between 0.1 and 0.3 per cent of the total population (Vowden et al., 1996), with an estimated 150 000 or more sufferers in the UK (Caring for the Community, Bandage Healthcare, 1994). According to Brown (1991), 'Treating leg ulcers is one of the most difficult and frustrating aspects of the work of district nurses. It has been estimated that we spend £600 million per year nationally treating this condition.'

Leg ulcers are slow to heal (some lasting for more than two years) and they frequently reoccur (Vowden et al., 1996): the cost of treatment is £2500 or more per patient per year (Caring for the Community, Bandage Healthcare, 1994). Not only do the wounds need sufficient cleansing, but also the underlying problem of improving venous return must be addressed for the wound to heal. If the wound area is treated with graduated compression, the wound will heal. Graduated compression is provided by compression bandaging, which is a major sector in the medical textile field with just under 2.5 million flat compression bandages sold every month (IMS Data, 1997). There are also many other associated dressings for treatment of leg ulcers and similar wounds available on the market, including paste bandages, four-layer bandages, tubular bandages and short- and long-stretch bandages.

Research Methodology

This case study was approached with a view to providing a snap shot study of RC and NPD within an organization, which would therefore provide a basis to develop a model of requirements capture suitable for an organization working in the traditional healthcare market. The information included in the case study was gained by a variety of research methods:

- In-depth interviews with key personnel, including the NPD director, NPD managers, technical director, director of hospital and community, product managers, the director of market research, and the directors of manufacturing. These personnel tended to be those who were involved in the NPD committee or worked on project teams for woundcare products.
- Observation exercises with sales representatives working out in the market place.
- Questionnaire of a cross-section of company personnel.
- Documentation relating to NPD, such as advertising material, process models, meeting minutes, proposal forms and design input briefs.

The Case Study Company

Bandage Group was established by an entrepreneur in the 1950s, when he developed ideas to market a tubular bandage. Then a range of elasticated tubular support bandages was launched, which revolutionized the method of bandage application for treatment of soft tissue injury. Since the 1970s, the group has developed its international network and their product range has been expanded, with acquisition and development of associated healthcare products, covering several major therapy areas, such as wound care, footcare and continence care.

New product Development at Bandage

Despite all the changes in the business over the last two years, the focus of woundcare and its related products still remains a core activity for Bandage. Bandage had been extremely successful in their growth through acquisition strategy, which began in 1987 with their first acquisition, gaining pace after the 1990 flotation. During this time, Bandage was purchasing many brands, relying on product line extension developments, rather than developing their own new products. A senior product manager for the company said: 'NPD is not particularly formal . . . A major strategic reason is that Bandage aquire products as opposed to developing them generally.'

During this time there were six new products launched, five of which were product line extensions. The new product was reasonably successful, but not to the extent that had been anticipated. Problems with the development and subsequent launch of Paste Aid coincided with a company-wide realization that they had outgrown the existing NPD function, which had previously operated as part of the technical department. Consequently, a new position of director of NPD was created. This director explained 'Because of the expansion of the company and the way the company was growing, they realized the need for a new position.'

The Medical Division

The Medical Division, which is responsible for marketing of wound care products, is split into Hospital and Community and is headed by the Director of Hospital and Community Products, working closely with Senior Product Managers. The split in the division is due to the different supply routes for each market (discussed in the next section of the case), although there is currently an attempt to bring the two sectors closer together and amalgamate the whole Division. This is a major factor in the shaping of the NHS, as there is becoming more of a focus on Primary care, which is care by nurses in the community, rather than patients being treated in hospital. The Medical Division focuses on wound care, compression therapy, dressing retention and continence care and is responsible for about one third of the Group's turnover. Bandage has several key competitors in these areas, who are more committed to NPD, which is included in part of their mission statement. 'A continuous process of supplying new and innovative products is supported by substantial R&D investment which includes the development of biological solutions to deliver new levels of healing.' (Annual Report, 1997). Understanding the structure of the healthcare market is vital for Bandage's strategic success, to enable the company to develop, launch and market products successfully. Bandage makes strong attempts to understand the market and incorporate this in its strategic approach. This can take on many guises, for example it can be in terms of understanding the structure of the market, monitoring government policies on healthcare and carrying out market research. This information is incorporated in to reports such as the business and launch plans. The UK healthcare market is fairly unique to other product markets, in that the main customer is the National Health Service (NHS). There are two main supply routes to the hospital sector and the community sector for Bandage to approach (see Figure 7.1).

Selling to hospitals in the UK is presently achieved through NHS Supplies (NHSS). NHSS can act in one of two ways. They can either act as an enabler on behalf of a trust, or trusts can buy directly from the NHSS wholesaling division. In their enabling capacity, NHSS can advise trusts on how to purchase groups of products, or they set up contracts, or they will do a bespoke tender for a trust. This may be the

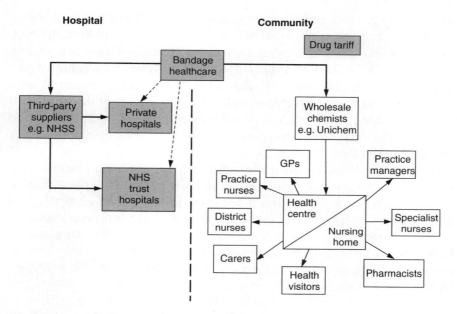

Figure 7.1 Supply routes for hospital and community
Source: Adapted from *Caring for the Community* Bandage Healthcare, 1994

main route for new products in to the NHS, as new products tend to go down this route before they are available through wholesale. Although NHSS would not recommend a particular company's products, they do have an overall picture of the marketplace and could make recommendations if asked. A buyer for NHSS explained: '...we may say this company is established and we know their delivery is alright and we've got their accounts, we've got all their quality control information and there's no problem there.'

NHSS and trusts have moved away from looking solely at price as a lead indicator for purchasing a product. A spokesman for NHSS said, 'What we actually go for is value for money.' NHSS will provide trusts with a service matrix showing price against delivery time, delivery methods, back-up stock, how long the company takes to respond to a technical query, where the product is manufactured and who makes them.

The other arm of NHSS is the wholesaling division, where thousands of products are stocked in warehouses across the country;

trusts can order directly from the warehouse. There are four major NHSS warehouses, eight smaller ones, and one trans-shipment point. NHSS warehousing is aiming constantly to drive down prices and eliminate cost from the supply chain. Their 1999 catalogue prices actually showed a price deflation of 0.12 per cent compared with 1998 prices, despite national inflation being 3 per cent. During 1998/ 99, the wholesaling division worked on a number of initiatives aimed at removing cost from the supply chain and improving efficiency (NHSS Annual Report, 1998/9).

Around 95 per cent of trusts take some level of service from NHSS, so it is important for Bandage that their products are available through this route. If they build up demand for a product that is not available through NHSS, there is little chance that the trust will choose another supply route to obtain it. According to the Director of Customer Care and NHS Contracts 'Hospital personnel may not be bothered trying to order nonstock products, as it is more time-consuming and they probably want the product immediately.' The Director of Customer Care and NHS Contracts at Bandage prioritizes the importance of the salesforce in stimulating demand in the hospital marketplace. He suggests that good demand will provide a sounder basis for negotiation with NHSS: '. . . there is no point in convincing NHS Supplies to stock your product if no-one orders it from the hospitals.' It is in this area that Bandage rely on their good name, for example, to introduce trials of new products in hospitals when other competitors may be trying to do the same, or to convince hospital personnel of the advantages of a Bandage product, and thus stimulate demand. For new products, it can be particularly difficult to negotiate with NHSS to stock the product. The director explains: 'This can't be done on the basis of sales figures so you have to do it on the basis of Bandage's size, commitment, history of previous deals, strength and knowledge.'

Bandage must maintain a good relationship with NHSS to enable their products to flow through the supply chain to the Trusts. 'NHSS will continue to be an important partner for Bandage in 1997/98 . . . An ongoing priority will be to build close business relationships with all members of the [NHSS] buying teams, and in particular, the new appointments.' (Bandage Medical Division, 1997/98). Bandage also has good relationships with the other third-party suppliers in the marketplace. These organizations act in the same way that NHSS do, but unlike NHSS are for-profit companies.

Selling in the community is achieved through a different supply route. Approximately 70 per cent of community products go to the large community wholesale chemists, who then supply retail chemists, of which there are about 12000 in the UK. Bandage supplies the large wholesaler chemists but, as in the hospital market, they stimulate demand for the products through targeting the customer, which in this case is community, district and practice nurses. The community market has become increasingly important for Bandage over the last few years as there becomes more of a focus on care in the community (after the publication of the Government white paper 'Caring for People' (1989), which emphasized community care). Community care has become more important as it is believed that patients would rather be cared for in their own homes rather than in hospital, and that the level of care would be better. It is also significantly cheaper (for the NHS) to provide care in a patient's home than in hospital (Caring for the Community, Bandage, 1994). Bandage have taken this in to account in forming their strategies. According to their Director of Hospital and Community, 'The latest [government] white paper is very clearly looking at primary care groups leading the way the health service is to be managed into the next ten years, and that really demands primary and secondary care to work together.' It is important that the salesforces for each sector work closely together, as the products used in hospitals are a strong influence on the choice of products used in the community. Although the majority of products cross over from hospital to community, not all those products used to treat patients in hospital are available for use in the community, an important factor for marketing. For example, according to one community nurse, 'Nurses refuse to use certain products despite being used in hospital. Problems arise from products not being on FP10. Maybe a patient is sent out of hospital with a product, but it cannot be used in the community.' (FP10 is the code given to a prescription that can be written in the community.) In other words, for a product to be successful in the community, a nurse has to be able to obtain the product with a prescription. Only certain products are available on prescription. These products are listed on the Drug Tariff, which is decided upon by the Department of Health. It can cause enormous problems for a company like Bandage if their product is not available on the Drug Tariff. It can delay the launch of a new product and reduce the potential sales of a product, which has been launched.

Sales and Promotion in the Healthcare Market

Bandage's main selling is achieved through their sales teams. Bandage sales representatives approach relevant personnel in hospitals, or in the community, e.g. at health centres and nursing homes. The representatives make some cold calls, but they also make appointments to see staff, often over lunch, where Bandage provides sandwiches and drinks as an incentive to the nurses. These meetings are often run as seminars, where staff are given information on therapy areas, followed by information about relevant Bandage products available for treatment in these areas. Free samples of the products discussed are provided, as well as various promotional gifts, such as pens and diaries bearing the Bandage product logos. Promotional leaflets are handed out detailing information on the products. The sales representatives also concentrate on building up relationships with the personnel they meet, by offering business cards so that they can be easily contacted, and sorting out individual problems, for example problems with availability of certain products from local chemists. Bandage has recently started an initiative of courtesy calls to inform local chemists of new products available, so that they know about them when a prescription is offered to them. Demand from customers, i.e. healthcare personnel, is the driving force in determining the competitive edge; building relationships between NHS purchasers and sales representatives is a key factor in stimulating demand for their products. Having sales representatives out in the market place also keeps up high awareness of the company and also Bandage products.

Communication between sales representatives and medical personnel is also very important, as it provides a two-way channel of communication between the company and their market; it is also a form of market research. Sales representatives can inform healthcare personnel of new product developments or advances in technology, which the staff, for example, may not have heard of or made time to read about. Healthcare personnel also give vital information and feed-

Name	Date		
Competitive activity i.e. contract prices and awards; price increases; new prods; literature; sales aids; clinical preference (with reasons); special offers; quality performance			**Action**
Product developments Ideas from cons. or any medical staff – however obscure			
Customer reaction to: Sales initiatives; quality; deliveries; pricing structure			

Figure 7.2   Bandage marketing department weekly report

back to the sales representatives, for example on existing products and what they may want from a new product.

The marketing department at Bandage provide all their sales staff with a weekly report, which is used to elicit first-hand information from the market (Figure 7.2). The potential for the information included in these reports could be massive. However, it appears that they are not utilized to their full potential. Information in the form of new product ideas may be formalized and passed on to the relevant marketing person. Product response issues, which are repeated, may be investigated with further market research. The reports are archived in an informal fashion. So, although certain points brought up in the weekly reports may be followed up, some opportunities may be missed as not enough people are seeing the full reports.

NEW PRODUCT DEVELOPMENT AT BANDAGE

The NPD process is led mainly by the technical department at Bandage. It is directed by the Bandage Control Sheet. The NPD committee consists of representatives from several departments at executive level (Table 7.1). The standard procedure for NPD is shown in Fig. 7.3 and described in detail in Table 7.2.

The membership of the NPD committee appears to be slightly unbalanced, with more technical-based members. Of particular interest is the absence of any representative of the salesforce, who are perhaps those closest to the customers, which raises the question of the role and use of weekly reports.

A formal procedure exists for NPD, but in practice the process is informal. Although it is stated that Bandage tries to have new products coming to fruition at staggered times, their NPD process appears to take a long time and not many products are launched. 'We usually endeavour to launch one or two a year; in reality that tends to be one rather than two and we do try to phase the programme over a number of years . . . ' (Director of hospital and community products, Bandage). The long product development cycle time is a consistent problem. Taking such a long time to market, as well as raising the cost of development, may also mean that requirements have changed during that time. One product manager at Bandage stated: 'I've been here two and a half years and not seen anything go from concept to launch.'

Table 7.1 NPD committee members at Bandage

Position
Deputy chief executive
Technical director
Marketing director, consumer division
Director of hospital and community products – Europe
Director of OTC contract sales
Director of hospital and community products
Director of market research
Director of operations – Oldham
Marketing controller – UK hospital division
Regulatory affairs manager
NPD manager, pharmaceuticals
NPD manager, medical devices
NPD manager, textiles
Technical manager

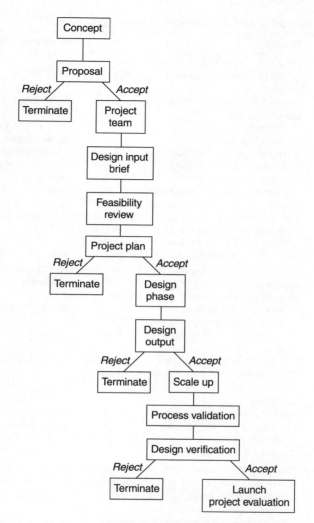

Figure 7.3 SP501 procedure flowchart for NPD at Bandage

The NPD committee oversees all the product development projects. They are responsible for allowing proposals to go into full-scale development and assess projects at each stage. It is the NPD committee who appoints a project manager to run each development. The project manager then appoints a project team, which usually consists of representatives from the major functions, particularly from techni-

Table 7.2   Details of NPD procedure at Bandage

Stage	Details	Responsibility
Concept	Idea for new product, design change or product copy suggested to NPD committee	Anyone
Proposal	Project proposal form is raised comprising of: 1. Product details 2. Proposal outcome 3. Development details 4. Environmental details 5. Marketing details On completion, form submitted to NPD committee for acceptance or rejection Projects may be instigated or terminated at the discretion of the technical director between NPD committee meetings, subject to ratification by committee	Originator of idea Technical director NPD manager/textile technologist Environment manager Marketing dept/market research NPD manager/textile technologist Technical director
Project team	Relative priority of approved subjects is established; project manager appointed who selects project team	NPD committee/project manager
	Individual progress record is initiated and updated throughout project to accurately record completion of each stage	Project manager
	List of key documents relevant to each stage is kept with individual progress record	Project manager
Design input brief	Covering Performance requirements Environmental requirements Cost requirements Timescale requirements	Project manager in liaison with project team
Feasibility review	Provides NPD committee with sufficient information to assess project viability	Project manager in liaison with project team
Project plan	Plan drafted to show all stages of project, e.g. • Resources/raw materials needed • Trials to be undertaken prior to release • Reporting stages and dates • Intermediate overall timing of project • Communication avenues and responsibilities Review; approve or reject	Project team NPD committee
Design phase	Regular meetings held to document progress Meetings minuted	Project manager

Stage	Details	Responsibility
Design output	Design output report generated to provide technical overview; compares prototype with design input brief Review; approve or reject	Project manager in liaison with Project team NPD committee
Scale up	Hold preproduction team briefing; minuted meeting of personnel involved with progressing in the preproduction trial in accordance with project plan; includes a member of the production planning department Preproduction trial used to determine: • Process capabilities • Quality standards • Accurate specifications • Work study details • Accurate costings etc.	Project manager in liaison with Production team Project team chaired by production team leader
Process validation	Process validation protocol and report issued	QA manager/production manager/project manager
Design verification	Prepared by comparing product produces in preproduction trial against design input brief Review; approve or reject Final specification issued Production co-ordinated by production planning department in conjunction with marketing department	Project team chaired by project manager NPD committee Technical department Production planning
Project evaluation	Completed postlaunch identifying areas of success and problems encountered	Project team chaired by project manager

cal and marketing. Although the director of market research is a member of the NPD committee, market research executives are not members of the project teams. The director of market research explains, 'The only involvement we might have with a project is if a member of the marketing team comes back from a meeting and says that they need some specific information from us.' The NPD committee meets approximately once every quarter. These meetings will last for about three hours and every development project is addressed, without necessarily being prioritized. This means that the NPD committee does not have the time to make considered decisions on each project, and have to move quickly to cover everything in the one meeting. The director of hospital and comunity products says: 'What happens at the moment is there's an agenda this long and everyone sits there and it's like "next, next, next".'

Between the NPD committee meetings, the project teams will have had several meetings and the project should have progressed forward. In reality, what seems to happen is that rather than having a continuum of work over the three months between meetings, there is a lot of work centred around the meeting. According to the director of operations, 'A hell of a lot of work goes into those meetings about two weeks before the meeting.' The technical director says: 'They [the project teams] do *not* have regular meetings, they are perhaps every two months.' Project teams do not have a specific schedule for meetings. Generally, they may occur every six weeks, although those involved are encouraged to continue working on the project even if the team has not met formally. 'Sometimes people have a tendency to wait until the next meeting to really talk to people in the group. We try to steer people away from that and say, "Look this can happen concurrently . . ." ' (director of hospital and community).

In theory, the project teams are responsible for preparing business plans, forecasts, design stages and so on, as part of the NPD process. The information fed into the NPD committee from the project teams should then enable the committee to make go/no go decisions at each of the stage gates. In reality, the stage-gate process is not followed at Bandage. Although it is generally felt that there would be no hesitation to withdraw development projects that are not going well, ('I think the Company is quite ruthless in kicking out the ones that we no longer see as important and focusing on the ones that are,' (director of operations)), the go/no go decision is not a formal one ('It is a largely subjective and emotive process,' (technical director)).

The whole process is led by the technical department, and NPD is actually a function of the technical department. For each new project, a project team is formed consisting of personnel from a variety of functions. However, the project managers are always from the technical department, so the process is not entirely market-orientated. The director of hospital and community says: 'I think we would often identify opportunities, which are then translated into something by the technical department, which we then can't accept or launch, rather than us perhaps driving the project and being more proactive.' This may be exacerbated by a lack of understanding by technical and marketing of each other's role and function. For example, the marketing department make full use of strategic tools, such as the Boston Consultancy Group Matrix, but the technical department has little or no idea of the value or use of these strategic tools. According to the technical director, 'They [strategic tools] are never used and are not well understood.' The technical department has a good knowledge of the market from sources such as journals, conferences, trade press, exhibitions and other publications, but they tend not to visit customers. Other information comes directly from the marketing department. Despite this, relationships between the technical department and marketing department have been described as 'generally good.'

REQUIREMENTS CAPTURE AT BANDAGE

RC is limited in the NPD process at Bandage. Although the company feels that including requirements is an integral part of the process, there are limited front-end activities, and the official NPD process begins only at the concept stage. There is no formalized process for RC. When asked how much time was spent on the early preconcept stages of NPD, the NPD director replied 'Very little before it gets into the system. Probably not enough or very little.' He went on to estimate that the overall time spent on these stages was probably about five to ten per cent of the overall time spent on any one development project.

Idea Generation

Potentially, anybody at Bandage can generate an idea for a new product. However, there is no formalized way of instituting idea generation. Anybody who has an idea for a new product should approach an NPD manager, who will assess the idea informally. If he or she thinks the idea has merit, he or she will fill in a project proposal form This is then be passed to the NPD committee, who complete the remaining sections relating to development details, including technical difficulty, availability of existing knowledge/equipment/facilities, development costs and time. This section is completed by the technical department, while marketing details, such as size of the market, target market, competitive details, possible market research needed and target price are completed by marketing/market research. This document constitutes the beginning of the NPD process at Bandage. Any idea that is generated has to go through this process to reach the NPD stage. However, not all ideas will reach this stage. If somebody comes up with a bright idea and approaches an NPD manager, the NPD manager can actually kill that idea immediately if he or she thinks it does not warrant merit. That idea will then never reach proposal form stage. The NPD manager said, 'An idea in its early stage could be assessed on gut feel and it's only when it starts going through the project proposal that it starts becoming formalized and we have a vision.'

Formalized idea generation techniques, which perhaps result in most ideas for NPD at Bandage, include brainstorming sessions, market need established through market research, and technical focus meetings that involve technical experts from the shop floor. Again there may be many ideas from these processes that never make it into a formal procedure. Rejected ideas are not assessed. Ideas that are suggested but considered not to have any merit are not even documented. Other ideas may be noted in memo form or as a file note. There is no specific way of returning to rejected ideas and appraising them. As the NPD director put it, ' . . . the only way to revisit ideas would be to go through old documents.'

Identifying Stakeholders

Customer/user requirements are considered to be an integral part of NPD at Bandage; however, there does not appear to be a clear understanding of who all the stakeholders are or how to assess their requirements formally. The NPD director said, 'The ones inside the company are fairly self-evident. The ones outside are recognized as being important over time.' The only method of assessing stakeholder importance is through additional market research. In terms of gaining information, this may be done by having regular meetings with internal stakeholders and talking to opinion leaders. The internal stakeholders are not identified formally, and some may actually be excluded, for example, the sales representatives, as mentioned earlier in the case. External stakeholders seem to be limited to opinion leaders, and perhaps customers and users. There is limited or no involvement of other external stakeholders such as competitors, suppliers, patients etc. Any involvement with stakeholders of this type tends to be ad hoc and depends on the project concerned. The NPD director explained: 'It may be that the initial idea came from a customer of from a supplier, or that we need to work very closely with a supplier to develop the product. It varies considerably. There's no hard and fast rule.' Suppliers are involved in NPD on some projects, but these, and other external stakeholders, are certainly not considered in a formal and integrated fashion.

Data sources such as journals, conference proceedings and other publications are used to feed information into personnel at Bandage.

The relative importance of the identified stakeholders is not assessed explicitly in terms of their relative importance to a particular project. Acording to the NPD director, the only way this may be done is through additional market research. This becomes apparent when the issue of requirements in the product development process arises. If requirements are included in the design brief and they cannot be met, '. . . you might have to go back and try and manipulate the results or manipulate the product or design. We design it so that it does or you have to consider the initial design brief.' (NPD director). This suggests that time may be wasted in trying to fix it so that the requirement of a relatively unimportant stakeholder is solved.

Bandage does not hold a database of stakeholders, although they do have a database of customers. An NPD manager said 'There won't be a database, but that sort of thing will be looked after by customer care people who might have a database.'

RC, as a part of the NPD process, is not clearly defined. There is no specific team that is responsible for putting requirements together or planning for RC. Other than the project team, who are responsible for filling in the design input brief, there is little evidence of RC. In terms of capturing requirements for a new product, the only method that may be implemented is a checklist to ensure that the obvious requirements are captured.

Information Gathering

Due to that fact that RC is not regarded as a process in itself, there is no information gathering that is specific to this process at Bandage.

Those involved in project teams may commission certain research from the market research department, which may be to discover requirements of certain groups, but they do not always set out with this in mind. Because the market research department does not have a direct link with NPD, they may find that they glean requirements information incidentally. This may include information that has not specifically been asked for, and may therefore never be fed in to the requirements gathering process. Internal information gathering may include brainstorming sessions. Externally, market research will carry out focus groups, interviews, product testing, user, task and environment analysis, competitor product analysis and concept testing. However, according to the director of market research, representative of market research do feel that they have a good channel of contact to feed back any interesting information that they may find incidentally: 'We have no problem at all with feeding back. It would normally be to marketing. We are very close to marketing and have no gap or wall to get across in terms of contact.'

Requirements Capture and New Product Development

Although there is a form of a phase review system in the NPD process at Bandage (see Figure 7.3), in reality this system does not work. The phase review is not carried out in a formal fashion; rather, 'it is a largely subjective and emotive process,' according to the technical director. Therefore, RC cannot be assessed formally through the NPD process. In terms of continuing RC throughout the NPD process, the only assessment that is carried out to ensure requirements are met is in the form of continually reviewing the design input brief. Again, this is not a formal process, and does not always work, so by the end of the NPD process, requirements that were set out at the start have not always been met.

A Model of Requirements Capture for Bandage

So far, we have examined the NPD process and RC activities at Bandage, and established that there is little evidence of successful RC. Any RC that does take place is very informal, dependent on the project concerned and carried out on an *ad hoc* basis. Although there have been many successful new products launched by Bandage, they have been aimed particularly at a short-term market. In order to improve long-term growth through new product launches, reduce time to market, decrease cost of development and improve the chances of success for new products, they need to implement a tighter NPD process and develop a model of RC.

Figures 7.4 to 7.10 show a model for RC that Bandage may use. It is broken down into sections for ease of explanations.

Figure 7.4 shows the use of specific idea generation techniques that involve more external stakeholders, for example through collaboration with suppliers or competitors, customers, users and market research. Internally, the model suggests more of a dissemination of the importance of ideas throughout the organization, so it is not necessarily limited to those managers involved in NPD, e.g. use of a staff intranet, suggestion box scheme and serendipity.

Figure 7.5 institutes a formal idea screening process, ensuring that *all* ideas are assessed formally. The screening process takes into account a variety of criteria relevant to the healthcare market to enable informed decisions to be made. An example of how this could be achieved would be to give each criterion a score on a scale of one to five: only those ideas that scored more than a certain number would go forward.

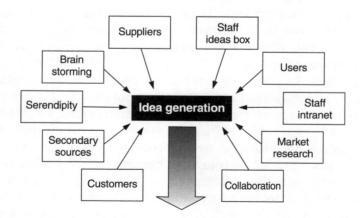

Figure 7.4   Idea generation model for RC at Bandage

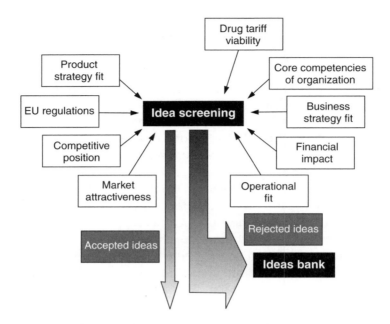

Figure 7.5   Idea screening model for RC at Bandage

Accepted ideas would move forward to the next stage, but instead of being filed and forgotten about, rejected ideas should be stored in an ideas bank. This should include the type of product, a description of the idea, the name of the person who originated the idea, and the reason why it was rejected. The purpose of this rejected ideas bank would be at least two-fold. Firstly, it would enable NPD managers to check new idea suggestions against old ones. If the idea has been rejected before, they would be able to find out why, and consequently save time on assessing the current suggestion either by rejecting it immediately or realizing that there is now an opportunity to be able to carry it forward. For example, the company may have invested in new machinery since the initial rejection, making the idea more feasible now. Secondly, the NPD manager may be able to go back to the originators to find out more information from them. This database, could have many other benefits, which may become more apparent through its use.

Figure 7.6   Stakeholder identification model for RC at Bandage

Figure 7.6 addresses the identification of stakeholders. This should be formalized so that *all* those involved with NPD are aware of who *all* the stakeholders are and why they are important. Another database should be set up to compile a list of the stakeholders. This should include names, positions, company, experience, area of expertise and previous involvement in NPD at Bandage. For any new product being developed, the NPD manager could gain access immediately to all the stakeholders relevant to that product category.

Once all the stakeholders have been identified, information should be gathered (Figure 7.7). This should be carried out using the relevant techniques, rather than being incidental to other market research that is being carried out. The company already has the capabilities for implementing techniques for gathering information, such as focus groups, interviews, product testing etc. However, those involved in carrying out this type of research should be more involved in the NPD process so that they have a clearer idea of the kind of information that is being fed into the process at all stages.

The information gathered should then be analysed in the normal way relevant to the information gathering technique used (Figure 7.8).

Figure 7.7   Information gathering model for RC at Bandage

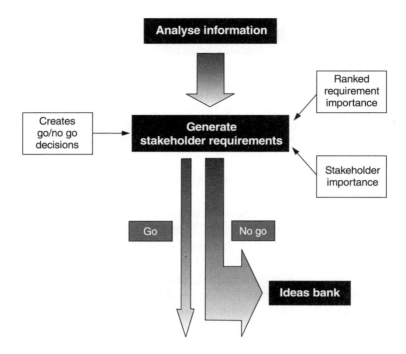

Figure 7.8   Information analysis model for RC at Bandage

This information provides details of all the stakeholder requirements needed. At this stage it is vital to attach importance to both the stakeholder and the individual requirements. This will enable the NPD manager to incorporate as many requirements as possible, particularly the most important requirements for success. Using a requirements matrix, to weigh up ability to deliver against relative importance will ensure the creation of strict go/no go decisions. At this stage, if ideas are rejected because their requirements could not be delivered, the rejected ideas should be added to the rejected ideas database, including a note explaining that they were rejected at this stage.

Once the relative importance has been attached to each requirement, the requirements can be analysed and the most suitable ones selected to be included in the product specifications (Figure 7.9).

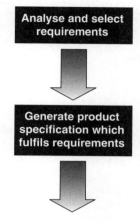

Figure 7.9   Requirements analysis model for RC at Bandage

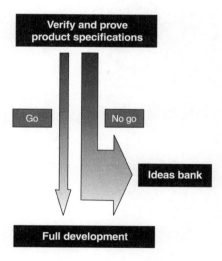

Figure 7.10   Specifications proof and verification model for RC at Bandage

Finally, each requirement should be presented in a more detailed fashion, including specific details, e.g. dimensions, components, availability and sources of raw materials (Figure 7.10). This will automatically create a further go/no go decision. Again, any rejected ideas can be added to the rejected ideas bank.

8

CONSTRUCT CASE STUDY

INTRODUCTION

Construct is a global manufacturer of power tools for the construction industry. Innovation is rare in the sector that Construct is based in, with the last major technological change occurring 40 years ago. A few years ago, an opportunity for NPD arose with changes in European health and safety legislation. The European marketing director of Construct recognized that new products appropriate for this legislation could open up new markets for the company. However, the company needed to move quickly to seize the markets before its competitors did.

European Design Centre

Construct was in the process of setting up a European Design Centre that was responsible for new products for Europe. However, when Construct decided to embark on this new programme, it had little expertise in NPD. According to the European marketing director, the company needed a starting point for the project: "We had nothing. We had no in-house experience of developing products from scratch. We had no supplier base. This has positive and negative benefits. Starting from fresh meant that we could do what we wanted; however the rest of management saw it as opening a can of worms as they weren't sure how it was going to work. It was not so much a decision as an acceptance that if we were to collapse the timeframe with a market-orientated product, there was no other way to be organized."

THE DESIGN TEAM

The European marketing director had the responsibility for setting up a design and development team, which had the aim to bring to market within 12 months, and within budget, a product in the 10-kg weight range that would be best in class for power, vibration and ergonomics. A number of questions were raised by top management.

- Could the company organize an efficient and effective design team?
- Who would be the members of the team?
- Would this team be able to manage the process having little experience of NPD?
- Would they be able to source external design expertise successfully?
- Would the project be to schedule, meet all customer requirements and still be within budget?

A small full team was put together consisting of representatives from marketing, design engineering. This core team was given sole responsibility for all the decisions concerning the project, and reported to a steering committee made up of directors of different functions. The marketing director notes that: 'Unless you give the team the authority to do the job, they won't take any of the responsibility for it. It helps get the motivation. By getting everyone in the room together it meant that everyone knew what was going on. We all believe that everyone can contribute to the design of the product, not just the engineers, and not just the core team members either.'

Each team member contributed on an equal footing. This meant that they bounced ideas between each other, giving different views on subjects that were not ordinarily within their traditional areas of expertise. Hierarchical forms of authority were also forgotten. Instead, project leader's duties were rotated amongst the group so that different people took command at different times.

Control was exercised through goal orientation, so that the team focused collectively on achieving tasks; satisfaction came from solving problems together, rather than individual conformity to meet a series of established milestones, or from subservience to an authority figure. The members of the team viewed their relationships with each other as being akin to a marriage; whilst there was bound to be conflict (since the free flow of opinions and ideas were encouraged), the members always made up afterwards!

THE STEERING COMMITTEE

A steering committee oversaw the team but, took no part in the team's decision making process. The committee could advise and guide the team, but not make any of the final decisions. Its responsibilities were to:

1. Set and concur with the team vision for the project.
2. Review change in the scope of the project.
3. Review changes in time, budgets and key product features.
4. Project status and milestones.
5. Remove strategic barriers.

The steering committee consisted of top management from finance, quality, purchasing and manufacturing, and the general manager. The core team and steering committee interacted closely throughout the project.

MARKET ANALYSIS

The type of information and the means of generating and collecting market information was planned carefully in order that an appropriate marketing strategy could be put together. The main areas that the team had to consider were:

- Market research that would generate product specifications, e.g. user needs, customer needs, industry regulation and legislation.
- Product positioning.
- Sales: past, present and predicted (and estimations of market size and value).
- Competitor information.

Market Research

Remaining close to the customer was an overriding concern of the product development team. Accordingly, the team worked closely with a core user group, which consisted of Construct's distributors, competitor's distributors, salespeople and end users.

The user group members (UGM) were compiled mainly from Europe, although support was also solicited from USA, Canada, South America, Asia and the Pacific Rim. The 50 to 60 members of the group were used to evaluate concepts and to verify that the product was on the right track in terms of the product specification's ability to satisfy market requirements. Most of the user information and specifications were compiled through close interaction with the UGM. Three approaches were used to talk to the UGM:

1. The UGM were asked for product feature preferences.
2. The UGM were then asked for direct requirements in order to create a wish list of product features.
3. Finally the UGM were asked what product features they disliked.

The team had difficulty in getting customers to articulate exact and precise needs in the abstract, so throughout the product development process, the UGM were shown a number of competitor tools (and in the final stages of the process, prototype tools) to elicit a better response. The team found that having tools in front of them to criticize tended to focus the UGM's attention on key issues.

Construct knew that health and safety features of power tools were becoming important as purchase criteria of their customers. This demand was driven primarily by health and safety regulations that were laid down to protect the end user. At the time, there was no regulation in force that limited the use of tools with a high level of vibration, but the pace of regulation in the industry, particularly in Europe, suggested that this would soon become an issue.

Competitive Analysis

Using competitive benchmarking, Construct categorized competitor products into a particular power/weight/vibration/cost ratio – low weight (in the 10-kg range), low vibration and low cost coupled with high power being the optimum for hand-held tools.

PROJECT CONSTRUCT

The marketing director realized at a very early stage that lack of in-house skills meant that suitable expertise would have to be bought into three areas: business, engineering and design. The team lacked industrial design skills, i.e. expertise that would make the product easy to use and appealing to the customer. Sourcing design expertise was not easy and Construct made a mistake with the first company it employed. From this experience, the team decided that its approach to the selection of design consultancy should follow certain criteria, as the marketing director explains: 'We wanted someone who wanted to come to the party. He had to take on some of the responsibility, and put his own stake in as well. If we fell, then we all fell together. We had the objective of starting a product design facility in Europe that went beyond this initial project. We wanted someone who was part of the team.'

At the same time, the design engineer had invented Vibra-Smooth – a vibration-reducing device that would give the product massive advantage over current competitor products, as the weight-to-power ratio was also improved. The inclusion of Vibra-Smooth would change the shape of the product radically, however, the detailed design of this device had still to be undertaken. Whilst the idea was proven in theory, it was unknown whether the device could work in practice or even be engineered into the product, along with a new body shell, within the allotted time.

This caused a major dilemma within the team. The Vibra-Smooth device would meet the customer requirement of less vibration. Should they try to incorporate this device into the product at the risk of missing the deadline, losing their market opportunity and potentially their market leadership position? Alternatively, perhaps it would be less risky to go into production, and try to sell the product without the vibration requirement, but to schedule?

Design Consultant

The team invited a number of design consultants to visit them and show their portfolios of work. From this, a design consultant was chosen. A design consultant aims to achieve the optimum design solution for the market, by working closely with client marketing and production teams during a design project. The consultant has the capability to manage projects from initial concepts through to production, dealing with many other design-related activities through-out the process.

The design consultant believed that design and development was the key to strategic market positioning of all successful products. For a specific target sector, it is vital to have the appropriate blend of appearance, function, economic manufacture and presentation.

Working with clients

The design consultant tries to establish at the beginning of a project a framework that defines the degree of freedom the consultancy can work within. However, this framework has to be flexible to allow for change in a product's development, and for this reason communication with the client at all times is seen to be key to a successful project. Awareness of the market requirements and the client's desires is critical. The design consultant describes how he works with his clients: 'You have to tell the client everything, otherwise at the end of the project, the product is not acceptable. This takes a lot of time, and typically we have put in more time than we wanted to.'

However, the vibration requirement had not been incorporated into the design and to date no decision had been taken to incorporate the device. The team welcomed the design consultant's views in this matter. With time pressing, the team needed a designer who was flexible, highly committed and could work quickly to design the product to schedule.

PROJECT CONSTRUCT DESIGN AND DEVELOPMENT PROCESS

The project was divided into four design and development stages:

1. Briefing
2. Feasibility study and detail design
3. CAD development
4. Rapid prototyping and tooling up.

Briefing

The briefing meeting was very informal, as the design engineer explains: 'What I'm looking for is a new image for the product. I don't just want the product to be a market beater functionally; I want our customers to be able to look at a product, and know it instinctively to be made by Construct.'

The team was still undecided as to whether to incorporate the Vibra-Smooth technology. Whilst some members of the core team wanted to apply some minor modifications to the existing prototype, others wanted to make use of the Vibra-Smooth device. Time was running out and the possibility of starting a new design was not viewed with particular relish given the pressure they were all under. Before making a final decision, the team welcomed some fresh input from the design consultant. Whilst the team described their requirements, the industrial designer made small thumb-nail sketches. The design engineer, commented later to the rest of the team that he was particularly impressed with the way the consultant put pencil to paper and started sketching in this initial discussion. This briefing was critical for a number of reasons, as the consultancy needed to know:

1. How the product was to be made.
2. The effect the additional Vibra-Smooth device would have on the internal geometry.
3. The type of materials and processes to be used for the moulding, and how they were to fit into the inner mechanisms.
4. Other existing Construct products, and how this new product was to fit into, or be a departure from, the existing range.
5. The critical elements in the design as perceived by the end user and customer.
6. Project management.

7. The number of units (as batches) to be produced in the first and second years.
8. The product handle configurations.

As the designer walked around Construct's factory, and was shown the existing product range, he soon realized that the product was going to be used in a fairly tough environment. The designer thought back to his student days. He had worked on a building site and on motorways during summer vacations and remembered the way the workmen had treated the tools, for example leaving the tools exposed to all weather conditions, and never cleaning them. The designer believed that these briefing situations were invaluable in absorbing the approach or the culture of the company.

Design Considerations

During the briefing process, the designer realized that the Vibra-Smooth device would give the product immense added value. If the device was to be included in the product, it meant a new product image and a change in dimensions so that, from an industrial design standpoint, they would have to start again. His view was that the Vibra-Smooth device should be included and he saw this as an opportunity to do something very different to any other product available in the industry. The team had to decide whether to spend longer to develop an innovative product, or to freeze the product and get it to market quickly. The team members held opposing opinions. Eventually they decided to support the radical redesign and incorporate the Vibra-Smooth device.

With the team united, the steering committee was convinced that this was the way forward, since their worry was that a me-too product would be developed. It was decided that an initial feasibility study conducted by the design consultancy would allow other possibilities to be explored. Aware that time was short, Construct had less than two weeks to come up with a conceptual design for the product.

Feasibility Study and Detail Design

A critical design consideration was that of the handle. The tool was to be used in a variety of situations and so interchangeable D- and T-shaped handles had to be available. The barrel of the tool, which tapered towards the pneumatic chisel, was the common component for each of the handles, so the best solution was to arrange a universal fixing system between the different types of handle and the main barrel, which was durable enough to withstand the environment in which the product was to be used. However, this meant that the fixings used to attach the handle to the barrel had to be hidden.

The Presentation

Following a two-week period, the designer produced some conceptual sketches. Aware of the time constraints, the designer homed in on one proposal. To illustrate his proposal, full-size two-dimensional representations were produced, along with a cardboard cut-out of the product for the core team to evaluate. Back-up sketches were also brought to the meeting.

When the colour illustrations were unveiled, the reaction to the concept from the core team was very positive. The designer's instincts were right, and the concept was considered for further development. What surprised the consultants was the reaction to the cardboard cut-out model. The design engineer remarked on how this gave a very clear indication of scale and the ergonomic problems involved.

The two companies discussed how to progress from concept stage to product development. The designer was asked to cost the components that made up the barrel housing and handles, and was given the name of the moulder and toolmaker, who had been sourced previously by Construct.

The European marketing director reiterated the time pressure on the project. He felt that this could not be stressed too much. Construct had already spent over nine months of their allotted time, and had another nine months to go. This meant that the exterior of the product had to be designed, developed and manufactured well within that timescale. The designer voiced his worry about proceeding from development to manufacture without a prototyping stage: 'How are we going to have time to produce an appearance model? It's important to realize that once we reach the tooling up stage, it's very difficult to change the design at that point and so it's far better to model the product now whilst the design is still on paper. Are you confident that the design will be exactly what you want?'

The designer had known other clients miss out this important stage in the development process and then regret it later on. However, Construct had already paid for a prototype from the previous consultancy and felt that, with time running out, it was best to proceed to full manufacture as quickly as possible. The European marketing manager knew that the earlier the product was produced, the more advantage it had over its competitors, and the higher price premium the market would be prepared to pay for it. He believed that the designer was able to visualize the product well enough without the need for an appearance model, and took the risk that the designer's expertise would avoid the need for another prototype.

Feasibility

As the designer started work on the external casing of the product, the design engineer was still, completing details for the Vibra-Smooth device and testing the product. The designer needed to stay in constant contact with the design engineer in case any significant developments occurred. He noted that: 'We received sketch drawings with general sizes of components, and where they fitted internally. Elements were still changing such as the diameter of the isolator and the barrel, because these were still being developed, and this affected the appearance obviously. That's the frustrating stage where things keep changing. Everything's fluid, but again, you have to expect that. It's a normal part of development.'

The designer knew enough about the moulding to produce some preliminary, detailed development drawings that would enable the toolmaker and moulder to put some more exact costs together. These drawings were done manually, but more detailed views had to be worked out using the designer's CAD software.

By the beginning of April, the team knew that all of the components would fit together without any problems. They knew how they were going to mount the internal components and the exhaust baffle had also been finalised. As the designer comments: 'We spent quite a lot of time detailing the bosses [where the bolts attaching the handle to the casing are located], and the rib sections that connected the bosses to the case, so a lot of the later development was to do with those sort of details. There was more work inside this moulding than there was outside.'

CAD Development

One of the reasons the designer was chosen by Construct was for his expertise with CAD/CAM (computer-aided design/computer-aided manufacture), and particularly rapid prototyping using a process known as stereolithography. The process of using such technology was divided into stages:

1. The design was developed to a detailed design stage in a similar way to the traditional design process.
2. The detailed development work was translated from a two-dimensional to a three-dimensional solid model using sophisticated CAD software (this development stage could have been reduced, or missed out entirely, if the product had been detail designed with CAD in the first place).
3. The CAD model was then loaded into a stereolithographic machine, which, through a chemical process, can reproduce physically the shape designed on computer.
4. The resultant shape was completed quickly by traditional model-makers and used by the toolmaker as a pattern. Using a spark erosion process, this pattern is used to form the metal injection moulding tool.
5. The moulder then used the tool to make the plastic moulds traditionally.

Whilst the designer produced all the information necessary for stage (1), other companies were subcontracted to create the three-dimensional model on computer, to produce the tools and to make the plastic moulds.

Rapid Prototyping and Tooling Up

Rapid prototyping was an expensive, but quick and effective, method of moving from drawings on paper to prototypes that could be used for the core mouldings for manufacture. The client had not used this approach before, because its cost had been prohibitive (conventional methods were slower but less than half the cost), but the urgency to move the product into the market rapidly justified the high cost. Indeed, one of the reasons for the client's choice of the designer was his ability to work with sophisticated technology in both the design and manufacturing process.

Before the product design could be finalized and put on to CAD, the design team, toolmakers and moulders had to reach agreement about the production method. A major consideration was whether to produce a one-piece moulding or a clam-shell arrangement (i.e. a mould that was in two halves). The former approach meant that the exterior of the product would be seamless but the production costs would be higher, because of the complexities involved. The European marketing director was adamant that the customers would prefer a flawless finish, and that any seams would appear as a product weakness, so the one-piece moulding route was taken.

The designer was anxious that the translation of the drawings into a three-dimensional shape was executed well; this involved continual liaison with the toolmakers. He noted that: 'The product may look a fairly simple thing, but it's actually tricky to model on computer because of some subtle blends and changes. Nonetheless, you rely on someone else's interpretation unless you are there the whole time. The point is that you can change a model on CAD quickly and easily because it's a virtual model.'

The major part of the design consultancy work finished once their drawings had been translated into the three-dimensional CAD model.

FROM DESIGN TO MANUFACTURE

The designer did not see the real design until the moulders were starting trial production runs. It was at this point that he noticed a small, almost unnoticeable, flaw with the exterior of the product: a slight ridge was apparent where the barrel body met with the end nozzle section. This had been caused purely by the CAD solid modelling process. When the company had translated the designer's drawings, the model had been divided into two separate sections and then 'joined' on screen. Because of the limitations of computer screen definition technology, the join looked perfect; transformed into a real solid model, the ridge became evident.

The designer was tempted to change the model to rectify the flaw: 'At the end of the day, there was so much time pressure the ridge remained, although it was feasible to take it out. When I went down to the toolmaker and saw the carbon electrode used to spark erode the tool, I really should have got some "Wet and Dry" [sandpaper], there and then and removed the detail. I think I would have been thrown out of the workshop if I had done that because it was a fairly traditional workplace! I think this is a good illustration of the process and its pitfalls. It's essential to have the designer right the way through the process.''

OUTCOME

The product was launched on time and was successful. The new Irgo-Pic demolition tool was designed to bring together power and comfort. Traditionally, powerful construction tools were heavy and uncomfortable to hold for any length of time and considerable hand and arm vibration was experienced by the user, which were health and safety risks. The product weighted 10 kg but delivered the performance of competitive 13-kg tools. This was achieved by an innovative design that combined advanced materials (polymers and plastics), engineering developments (Vibra-Smooth isolator) and ergonomic design (grip areas and handle to spread force, reduce stress and give protection to the operator's hands). The product became a world leader.

SECTION THREE
Guidelines to Requirements Capture

9 REQUIREMENTS CAPTURE PROCESS

This section provides practical guidance on the process of RC. It describes the main aspects of the requirements process, and the stages and activities which need to be undertaken.

REQUIREMENTS CAPTURE OBJECTIVES

The objective of an RC process is to create a consistent set of information that represents the composite views of all stakeholders. For the purposes of these guidelines, we refer to this information as the composite requirements specification (CRS), and define it as the information required for a product to meet stakeholder, technical and design requirements. The CRS will contain information that many businesses may currently record in three separate documents: market requirements specification; system requirements specification; and product requirement specification. It is suggested that such information be amalgamated into a single database, preferably held on the business's IT system.

Developing a successful CRS depends on the following activities:

1. Defining comprehensively and objectively the stakeholders in the product concept.
2. Considering external trends that may influence the requirements, such as technology.
3. Gathering information and requirements from stakeholders and information sources.
4. Analysing gathered information and requirements.

THE REQUIREMENTS CAPTURE PROCESS

RC activities and their outputs during the initial stages of the product development process are outlined in Figure 9.1. This figure describes the early process of NPD. RC for product development begins in phase zero, or stage zero, of an NPD process; it is here that ideas are generated and identified.

During phase one (concept testing), initial RC is performed to flesh out and better understand the product concept. This allows a decision to be taken on whether to proceed further and commit more resources, or drop the concept (phase one review).

In phase two (feasibility study), more extensive RC is undertaken to enable the formulation of a detailed product specification.

The two critical targets for an RC process are that at least 85 per cent of RC *effort* must be expended, and at least 85 per cent of the final requirements for the product under development must be *defined before the end of Phase 2*.

After idea generation, the RC process, which takes place in phases one and two can be divided into the following seven areas:

1. Idea screening
2. Stakeholder identification and assessment
3. Planning for RC
4. Information and requirements gathering
5. Information analysis
6. Composite requirements specification
7. Requirements analysis.

Idea Screening

Ideas submitted for product development should be screened regularly against key criteria. Passing through this initial filter – phase zero review – is crucial. Product concepts should not be railroaded through, or allowed to bypass this stage gate.

Detailed assessments of return on investment are unproductive at this very early stage. More appropriate is a scheme based on general strategic and financial considerations, or criteria such as that given in Table 9.1.

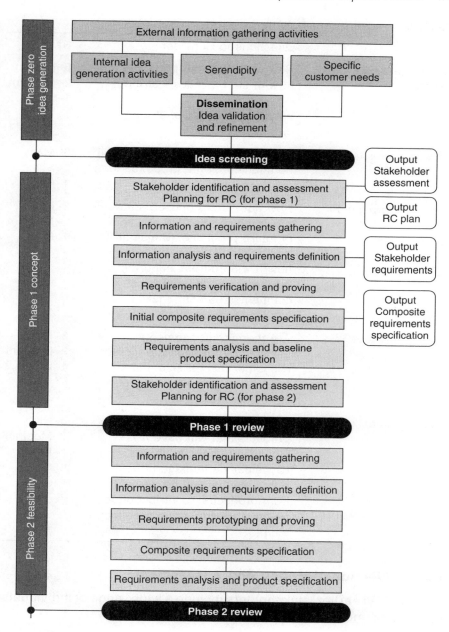

Figure 9.1   RC activities

Table 9.1   Idea screening criteria

Criteria	Questions to Consider	Rank
Fit with business strategy	How well does the proposed idea fit with the business's strategy? What is the sense of strategic urgency?	3–High 2–Medium 1–Low
Fit with product strategy	How many planned products will be affected by the proposed idea?	3–Many 2–Some 1–Few
Competitive position	How does the proposed idea affect the competitive position of future products? (Consider magnitude of proposed idea, how it will address important customer needs, number of companies that can make similar products, etc.)	3–High 2–Medium 1–Low
Market attractiveness	Are the market segments targeted by the idea attractive? (Consider market size, market growth rate, market share of top competitors, etc.)	3–High 2–Medium 1–Low
Financial impact	Will the proposed idea result in products that will have a significant financial impact? (Consider percentage of business revenues that will be derived from product(s), contribution to revenue growth, price premium, etc.)	3–High 2–Medium 1–Low

Stakeholder Identification and Assessment

As described earlier, stakeholders include a wide range of individuals and groups, including:

- external stakeholders (suppliers, distributors, customers);

- internal stakeholders (all internal functions including personnel and finance); and
- data sources (books, documents, media).

The particular stakeholders that relate to a product development project must be identified at an early stage. The characteristics of these stakeholders are then assessed.

Identifying stakeholders

When identifying stakeholders for RC, the following points must be remembered:

- The requirements of stakeholders from all countries in which the product will be sold must be considered.
- The various categories of stakeholders (including those who will not play a part in buying) must be considered.
- The characteristics of each stakeholder must be identified and recorded.
- Each stakeholder type's physical, organizational and technical environment must be identified.
- Potential data sources (individuals or groups that are knowledgeable on the subject who, while not direct stakeholders, may influence product development) must be identified.
- Each stakeholder's importance to the success of the product development must be accounted for.

Assessment

Once identified, stakeholder characteristics must be defined clearly. A number of factors must be considered, including:

- relationship to product concept;
  - potential/existing customer
  - potential/existing user
  - potential/existing supplier
- Organizational environment;
  - type of organization

- size
- culture (e.g. risk taking, risk averse)
- physical environment – type of workplace;
- technical environment – high or low tech?
- relationship to business;
    - past collaborator in product development
    - past/current customer
    - past/current supplier
    - friend of employee
- individual stakeholder
    - role in organization
    - level of influence
    - objectives.

The significance of particular stakeholders to the success of the product development must be taken into account to enable the subsequent ranking of captured requirements. To this end, stakeholders allocate a weighting between one and five, which relates to their importance to the project. This information should be recorded, either as a document or, ideally, in a computer database. In this way, a stakeholder archive can be built up allowing information to be reused in multiple development projects. An example of a stakeholder assessment entry in such a database is given in Figure 9.2. This particular stakeholder, a potential customer, was given a weighting of four.

Planning for Requirements Capture

It is important during product development that RC is well planned in order to:

- clarify objectives and define the outcomes;
- formulate activities to achieve the defined outcomes;
- allocate responsibilities;
- allocate time and resources;
- enable those involved to be briefed clearly;
- ensure that the RC process runs smoothly.

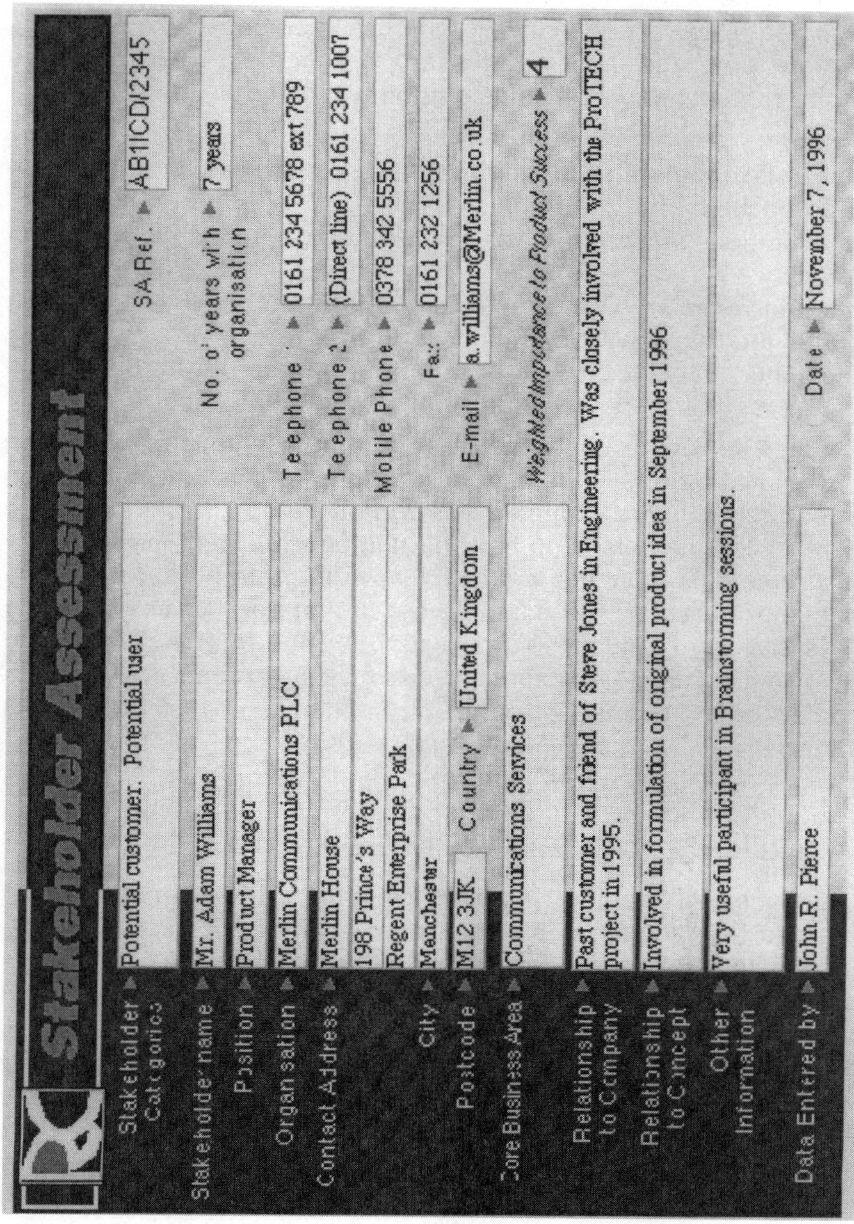

Stakeholder Assessment

Stakeholder Categories	Potential customer. Potential user
	SA Ref. ▲ AB1ICDI2345
Stakeholder name	Mr. Adam Williams
Position	Product Manager
	No. of years with organisation ▲ 7 years
Organisation	Merlin Communications PLC
Contact Address	Merlin House
	198 Prince's Way
	Regent Enterprise Park
City	Manchester
Postcode	M12 3JK Country ▲ United Kingdom
	Telephone ▲ 0161 234 5678 ext 789
	Telephone 2 ▲ (Direct line) 0161 234 1007
	Mobile Phone ▲ 0378 342 5556
	Fax ▲ 0161 232 1256
	E-mail ▲ a.williams@Merlin.co.uk
Core Business Area	Communications Services
	Weighted Importance to Product Success ▲ 4
Relationship to Company	Past customer and friend of Steve Jones in Engineering. Was closely involved with the ProTECH project in 1995.
Relationship to Concept	Involved in formulation of original product idea in September 1996
Other Information	Very useful participant in Brainstorming sessions.
Data Entered by ▲	John R. Pierce
	Date ▲ November 7, 1996

Figure 9.2   Example of a stakeholder assessment

To help achieve this, a requirements capture plan (RCP) should be formulated. This describes the RC process to be undertaken in terms of people, time and money necessary to achieve a comprehensive plan. Its contents should include the following:

- the stakeholders and information sources who are to be approached;
- the methods that are to be used to gather information and requirements;
- the individual who is going to perform the RC activity;
- when the RC activity is to be performed;
- how much it will cost.

There is no rule or best practice regarding how long or how short the RCP should be. What is important is that the relevant information and requirements are collected from the identified stakeholders. The RCP must contain details on how this will be achieved. The plan may be a written document but, again, it would be preferable to hold it on a computer database. An example of the first page of an electronic RCP is shown in Figure 9.3. It is usual that the RCP is refined and updated during the development process, as the product specification becomes better defined and the information needs of the project change.

Information and Requirements Gathering

As described in Chapter 3, various methods can be used to gather information and requirements. Information can be elicited from stakeholders and information sources using questionnaires, interviews and group discussions, or in response to product descriptions and prototypes. The methods used will vary according to the type of product, sources of information, access to stakeholders and stage in the development process. For example, qualitative research is extremely useful at the exploratory front end of the development process. It is usually necessary to use more than one method. In general, the more innovative the product, the more effort should be made to establish the many stakeholders' requirements. More detailed information

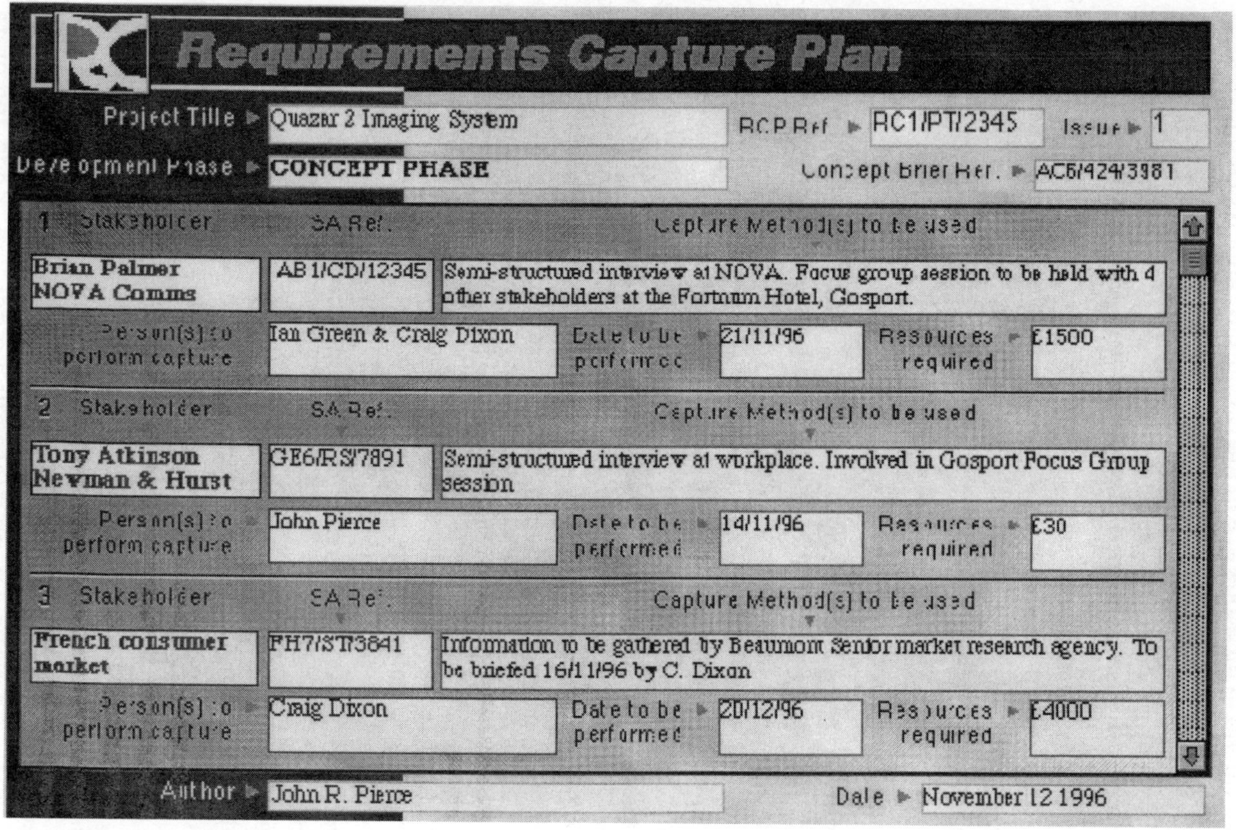

Figure 9.3 Example of an RCP

regarding these methods are in the Capture methods discussed at the end of this chapter.

Information Analysis and Requirements Generation

Information and requirements gathering often results in a wealth of data. This should be analysed systematically to develop a knowledge base and to clarify the most relevant and appropriate requirements. It is also necessary to minimize risk.

Risk minimization

By analysing and understanding the data collected during the requirements gathering phase, the risk of problems occurring in the development project can be minimalized. Obviously, it is not always possible to quantify the way in which factors such as future market changes or competitor activities will impact on the development project, simply because there may be no quantifiable data available. However, it is often found in retrospect that although the necessary information *was* available, its meaning and value were not recognized at the time. Consequently, it is necessary to use critical thinking and creativity in processing the available information, and to get feedback from stakeholders and information sources on those issues for which there is no quantifiable data. This crucial data analysis activity is best performed in a group context where the meanings of data and the results of information capture activities can be discussed and the appropriate requirements defined. The analysis of data and the definition of requirements should not be performed by just one or two people.

Requirements can be written down in the form of descriptive statements. For example, the requirements for a mobile phone may range from ''the product should reflect sophistication'' to ''the structural shell shall be of no more than two injection-moulded components''.

Stakeholder requirements

All stakeholder requirements generated from the careful analysis of the gathered data (including information regarding needs and preferences) must be recorded formally. This may be done by entering the information on individual stakeholder requirements forms or, if available, adding it to a stakeholder requirements database. Where possible, each requirement should be given a weighting by the stakeholder, reflecting how important that requirement is to them (1 = low, 5 = high). Product needs and requirements requested specifically by a stakeholder should also be indicated in some way. Recording this extra information allows individual product features to be traced back to specific stakeholders, and informs the future trade-off decisions that will invariably take place at a later stage in development. The information contained in this database can be added to, and updated, as requirements refinement continues, and represents the results of information capture for each stakeholder individual, group and organization. An example of an entry in a stakeholder requirements database is shown in Figure 9.4.

Composite Requirements Specification

All requirements that have been gathered from the various stakeholders and information sources are listed in the composite requirements specification along with two weightings:

- the relative importance of each requirement to project success; and
- the relative ability of the development programme to deliver each requirement on schedule and to cost.

An example of a composite requirements form is given in Figure 9.5. These two weightings are important in that they enable the requirements to be ranked in order of importance and company ability to deliver.

Relative Importance

This figure is the average of the weightings (importance to product success) assigned to all the stakeholders supporting a particular requirement, and their ranking of that requirement.

Figure 9.4   Example of a stakeholder requirements record

Composite Requirements Secification

Projected Title	PAGE	OF
TOPAZ 4 Network System	1	6

Author(s)	CRS Ref.	Issue
Graham Manning	MM2/CF/8934	1
Susan Fletcher	ID Ref.	
David Gibson	DR6/KT/1164	

REQUIREMENT DESCRIPTORS	RELATIVE IMPORTANCE ▼	ABILITY TO DELIVER ▼
.... *Requirement descriptor a*	4.8	2
.... *Requirement descriptor b*	4.8	4
.... *Requirement descriptor c*	4.8	3
.... *Requirement descriptor d*	4.7	3
.... *Requirement descriptor e*	4.6	2
.... *Requirement descriptor f*	4.6	5
.... *Requirement descriptor g*	4.4	3
.... *Requirement descriptor h*	4.4	5
.... *Requirement descriptor i*	4.4	5
.... *Requirement descriptor j*	4.4	4
.... *Requirement descriptor k*	4.3	2
.... *Requirement descriptor l*	4.1	1
.... *Requirement descriptor m*	4.1	3
.... *Requirement descriptor n*	4.0	3
.... *Requirement descriptor o*	4.0	4
.... *Requirement descriptor p*	3.9	1
.... *Requirement descriptor q*	3.9	2
.... *Requirement descriptor r*	3.8	5
.... *Requirement descriptor s*	3.8	2

(continued)

PROPOSED	SPONSORED	AUTHORISED
Signature	Signature	Signature
Position Project Manager	Position Project Group Mgr	Position Marketing Director
Date	Date	Date

Figure 9.5   Example of a composite requirements specifications form

For example, suppose there are five stakeholders who give information leading to the requirement, 'the product shall be discreet'.
Using the data entered in the stakeholder requirements database,
the weighted importance to product success of each stakeholder is
added to their ranking of the particular requirement. The mean of
these figures is the *relative importance* of that requirement. An example is given in Table 9.2.

The relative importance of the requirement, *"the product shall be
discreet"*, is therefore 5.8.

Ability to deliver

This figure is an estimate of the ease or difficulty of fulfilling a specific
requirement. It should take into account the resources available as
well as time constraints.

A scale of 1 to 5 can be used, as follows:

1. Not possible to achieve.
2. Difficult to achieve (may incur extra costs).
3. Achievable.
4. Easily achievable.
5. Very easy to achieve.

The ability to deliver figure should be entered in the composite
requirements specification as early in the development as possible.
During the very early stages of development, this figure will be a

Table 9.2 Example of stakeholder weightings

Stakeholder	**A** Importance of stakeholder to product success	**B** Stakeholder ranking of requirement	**A + B**
1	2	3	5
2	2	2	4
3	3	2	5
4	5	4	9
5	2	4	6
Relative importance of requirement (mean)			**5.8**

'guesstimate', but as requirements are developed and refined it should become more accurate.

Scope

When determining the scope for a composite requirements specification, technical and logistical issues must be considered. For example:

- Are the features within the proposed products compatible? (i.e. are feature interactions defined?)
- Can the proposed product function or interface with other products within the portfolio of the business? (i.e. are product interface dependencies defined?)
- Are related projects co-ordinated to synchronize delivery of compatible systems? (i.e. are interproject dependencies defined, agreed and managed through project management plans?)

Requirements Analysis

The two weightings, relative importance and ability to deliver, can be combined in a requirements analysis matrix.

Requirements analysis matrix

A requirements analysis matrix is shown in Figure 9.6.

Requirements can be plotted on to the matrix to give an overview of the total requirements for a development project. The four quadrants of the matrix can be considered as follows:

Quadrant 1
Relative importance = High
Ability to deliver = High

This quadrant contains the requirements that are most likely to form the product specification.

Quadrant 2
Relative importance = High
Ability to deliver = Low

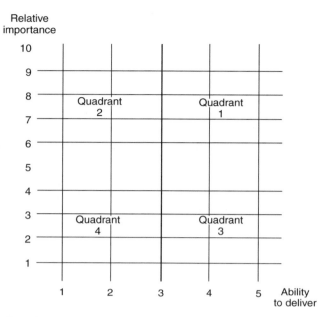

Figure 9.6   Requirements analysis matrix

Quadrant 3
Relative importance = Low
Ability to deliver = High

While being easily fulfilled, requirements in this quadrant are not particularly important to project success. Such requirements may be incorporated into the product specification if it is considered worth the expense (e.g. to aid the product's differentiation from others in the market). In some situations, it may be considered a better use of resources to drop such requirements and concentrate on those in quadrants 1 and 2.

Quadrant 4
Relative importance = Low
Ability to deliver = Low

Requirements in this quadrant should not normally be pursued, as their low importance does not justify the expense their realization would entail.

It must be stressed that the use of such a matrix to analyse any requirement is only as valid as the values for relative importance and ability to deliver assigned to it. Regarding the second of these weightings, there are two important situations when this figure may indicate the need for further investigation: an ability to deliver figure of 1 (not possible to achieve) or 5 (very easy to achieve).

An ability to deliver score of 1 may indicate the need for further study of a requirement and for creative thinking. By attempting to define the requirement more closely, it is possible that an alternative, more easily achievable, requirement may be found. To take a simple example, the stakeholder requirement that '*the office should be larger*' may be unachievable because of the physical constraints of the building in which it exists. However, research into what forms the basis of this requirement shows that it stems from stakeholders feeling that the office is dark and claustrophobic. Rearranging the office space, cleaning the windows, and painting the walls a light colour is obviously much more achievable. However, it also changes the stakeholders' perceptions and fulfils, indirectly, the original requirement.

Although an ability to deliver score of 5 might seem an ideal situation, it may indicate that the requirement is the result of stake-holders not understanding (or not being allowed to consider) the full range of what is possible, This is especially true when dealing with new-to-the-world and highly technologically complex products. In such situations, it may be useful to attempt to enhance the requirement and then validate it through repeat testing with the stakeholder. The results of such requirement enhancement may include:

- indirectly producing ideas for a new product development and incremental development;
- the design of a more attractive and competitive product; and
- increased product differentiation from competitors in the same market area.

RESPONSIBILITY FOR REQUIREMENTS CAPTURE

There are three main areas of responsibility for RC:

- It is the responsibility of everyone in the business to come up with ideas for potential new products and product improvements.
- It is the responsibility of all those involved with customers and in product development to capture stakeholder requirements.
- A third area of responsibility relates to a group of individuals known as the *requirements capture group.*

Requirements Capture group

The requirements capture group is the marketing-led, multiskilled group that is responsible for the predevelopment, phase zero activities that take place within the business. Membership of this group may include individuals from key areas such as strategy, business planning and other major business functions. The group is responsible for maintaining the ideas bank – the archive in which all product development ideas generated are stored – as well as disseminating these ideas throughout the business to allow their discussion, validation and refinement. The requirements capture group is also responsible for the screening of ideas at the preconcept phase (phase zero).

The requirements capture group's responsibilities include:

- Undertaking and/or commissioning both ad hoc and planned market research.
- Maintaining and managing the database of ideas and information for use by the rest of the business.
- Publishing a regular bulletin or newsletter to disseminate ideas for discussion and validation.
- Developing market plans and supporting business cases.
- Screening ideas and concepts at phase zero.

10   INTEGRATING REQUIREMENTS CAPTURE WITH PRODUCT DEVELOPMENT

INTRODUCTION

RC must be considered throughout the product development lifecycle, from gathering stakeholder requirements and information, generating the product specification, and refining and validating the product requirements, through prototyping, to customer feedback on the finished product.

RC plays an important role in the generation of product ideas at the preconcept stage. Although we focus on the preconcept, concept and feasibility stages (phase zero to phase two), RC continues, to a lesser extent, throughout the lifecycle. The RC process can therefore be mapped directly on to the seven-phase stage gate development process giving an eight-phase process:

0.   preconcept: idea generation and screening
1.   Concept testing
2.   Feasibility study
3.   Development and integration
4.   Testing and field trial
5.   Product launch
6.   Ongoing performance review
7.   Product withdrawal

Figure 10.1 provides an overview of the actions involved in the RC process, and shows how these are integrated into the phase review

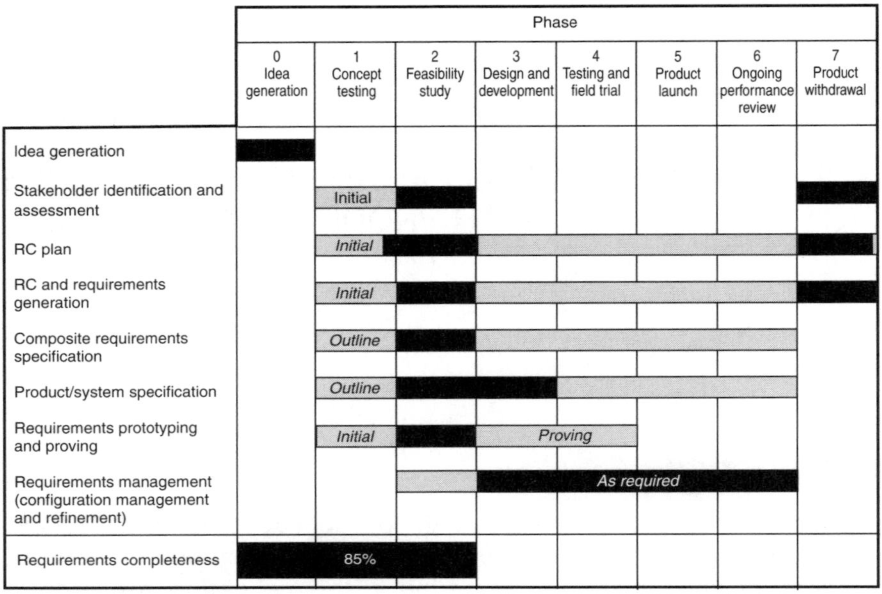

	Phase							
	0 Idea generation	1 Concept testing	2 Feasibility study	3 Design and development	4 Testing and field trial	5 Product launch	6 Ongoing performance review	7 Product withdrawal
Idea generation	■							
Stakeholder identification and assessment		Initial ■						■
RC plan		Initial ■					■	
RC and requirements generation		Initial ■					■	
Composite requirements specification		Outline ■						
Product/system specification		Outline ■						
Requirements prototyping and proving		Initial ■	Proving					
Requirements management (configuration management and refinement)			As required					
Requirements completeness		85%						

Figure 10.1   Overview of RC actions in the product development lifecycle

process. Exactly how the RC process integrates with the broader product development lifecycle must be tailored to suit the way the business operates. Nevertheless, a generic approach to integrating RC with the early stages of the product development process – phase zero to phase two – can be outlined. The next section defines the activities of the early phase of the NPD process, the deliverables and the goals.

PHASE ZERO: IDEA GENERATION

Before Idea Screening

1. Generate idea.
2. Create one-page idea description.
3. Disseminate idea.
4. Refine and enhance idea if necessary.

Deliverables

One-page idea description.

Goals

1. Generation of idea.
2. Definition of outline product idea.
3. Discussion, validation and enhancement of idea within business.
4. Authority for further RC, or reject.
5. Log details onto database.

A summary of the RC process for phase zero, including roles, activities and responsibilities, is given in Figure 10.2.

PHASE ONE: CONCEPT TESTING

Phase One: Actions

1. Create a requirements capture plan (RCP) to outline the activities that will take place in phase one. This includes:
   - Identification and assessment of stakeholders in the proposed product concept.
   - Capture methods to be used.
   - Which individuals will perform these capture activities?
   - When they will be performed?
   - What resources are required?
2. Gather stakeholder information to define requirements.
3. Verify and validate stakeholder requirements.
4. Create outline composite requirements specification (CRS).
5. Analyse requirements and create outline product specification.
6. Assess stakeholders and create refined RCP (RCP issue 2) for use in phase two.

Deliverables

1. RCP for phase one, which includes stakeholder assessment (SA).
2. Outline stakeholder requirements.
3. Outline composite requirements specification (CRS).

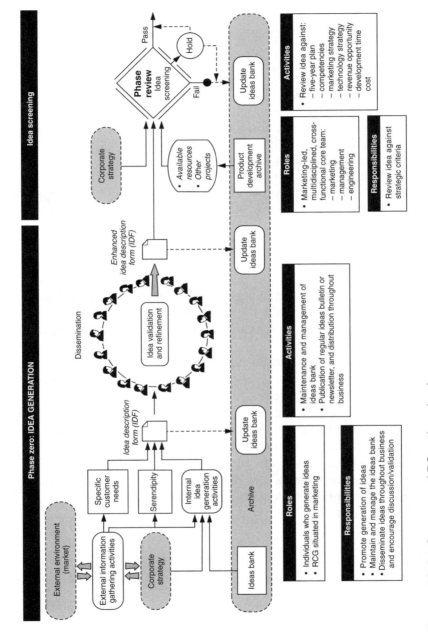

Figure 10.2   Summary of RC actions in phase zero

4. Outline product description.
5. Detailed RCP for phase two, which includes:
    *   refined stakeholder assessment (SA);
    *   capture methods to be used;
    *   which individuals will perform these capture activities;
    *   when they will be performed; and
    *   what resources are required.

Goals

1. Generation of an outline CRS and, from this, an outline product description.
2. Definition of a detailed RCP for phase 2.
3. Authority for further RC.

The result of the review after phase one may not be simply pass or fail. There may be situations where it is judged inappropriate to proceed until further RC has been carried out, or until amendments are made to the proposed requirements capture plan for use in phase two.

Again, fails at this stage must be viewed as positive. The aim is not simply to get the concept to the next stage, but to truly test the concept against the captured information. Failure is not a reflection of poor performance, but most often indicates that the concept testing phase has fulfilled its function, and prevented the business from making an inappropriate investment of time and resources.

A summary of the RC process for phase one, including roles, activities and responsibilities, is given in Figure 10.3.

PHASE TWO: FEASIBILITY STUDY

Phase Two Actions

1. Gather stakeholder requirements and information to define requirements.
2. Implement the RCP.
3. Verify and validate stakeholder requirements.
4. Create refined CRS.
5. Analyse requirements and create product specification.
6. Prove requirements.

Figure 10.3 Summary of RC actions in phase one

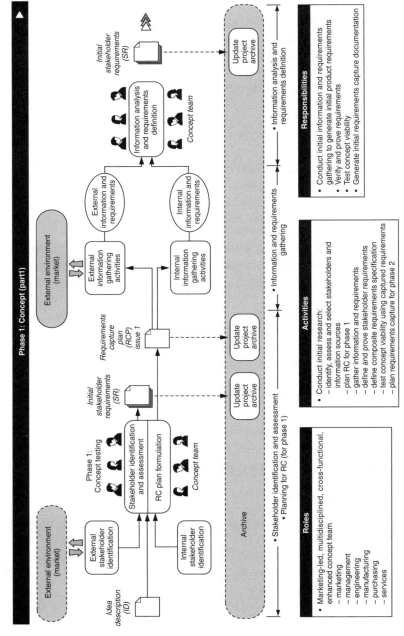

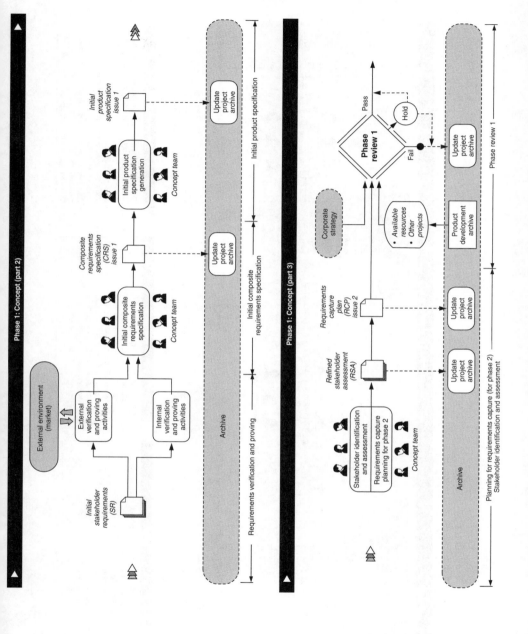

Phase 1: Concept (part 2)

External environment (market)

Initial stakeholder requirements (SR)

External verification and proving activities

Internal verification and proving activities

Initial composite requirements specification

Concept team

Composite requirements specification (CRS) issue 1

Initial product specification generation

Concept team

Initial product specification issue 1

Update project archive

Update project archive

Archive

Requirements verification and proving

Initial composite requirements specification

Initial product specification

Phase 1: Concept (part 3)

Stakeholder identification and assessment

Requirements capture planning for phase 2

Concept team

Refined stakeholder assessment (RSA)

Requirements capture plan (RCP) issue 2

Corporate strategy

Phase review 1

Pass

Hold

Fail

- Available resources
- Other projects

Update project archive

Update project archive

Product development archive

Update project archive

Archive

Planning for requirements capture (for phase 2)
Stakeholder identification and assessment

Phase review 1

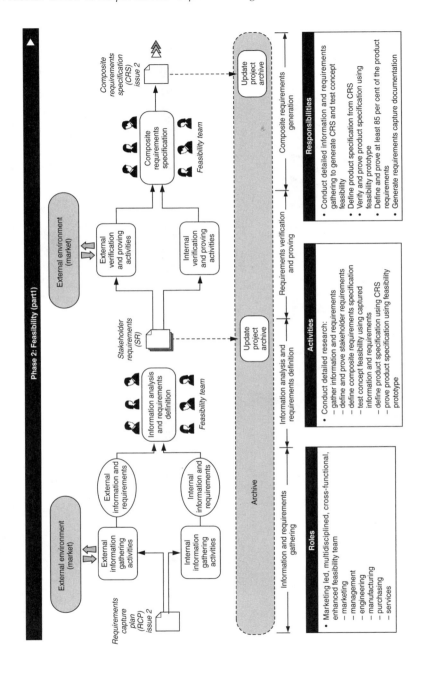

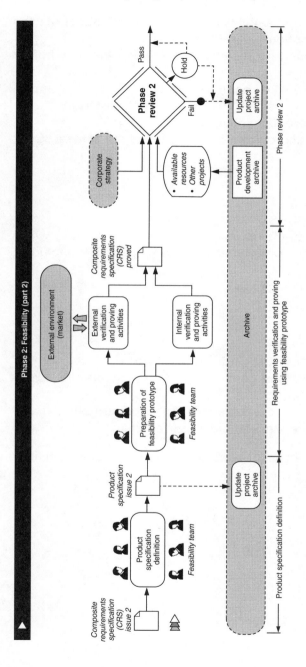

Figure 10.4 Summary of RC actions in phase two

   i Prepare and run a feasibility prototype to verify and prove the product specification.

  ii Revise the product specification until it meets the stakeholder needs.

 iii Revise the composite requirements specification as appropriate.

 iv Create refined product specification.

  v Repeat until finial requirements for product are at least 85 per cent defined.

Deliverables

1. Refined and proved CRS.
2. Completed requirements capture plan for phase two, which includes feasibility prototype/validation results (including usability).
3. Detailed product specification.

Goals

1. Implementation of the RC plan for phase two.
2. Definition of the CRS and confirmation that it meets the appropriate stakeholder needs.
3. Definition of the product specification and confirmation that it fulfils the appropriate stakeholder requirements.

A summary of the RC process for phase two, including roles, activities and responsibilities, is given in Figure 10.4.

REFERENCES

Allen, T. (1977) *Managing The Flow of Technology,* MIT Press, Cambridge, Mass.

Anderson, R.E. (1993) 'HRD's Role in Concurrent Engineering,' *Training & Development* **47** (6): 49.

Baden Fuller, C. (1995) 'Strategic Innovation, Corporate Entrepreneurship and Matching Outside In to Inside Out Approaches to Strategy Research', *British Journal of Management* **6** (December, special issue).

Bailetti, A.J. and Guild, P.D. (1991) 'A Method for Projects Seeking to Merge Technical Advancements with Potential Markets', *R&D Management* **21** (4): 291–300.

Barczak, G. (1995) 'New Product Strategy, Structure, Process and Performance in the Telecommunications Industry', *Journal of Product Innovation Management* **12**: 3–15.

Bissell, J. (1998) 'Product Innovation: Marketers' Task, Too', *Brandweek* **39** (27): 22.

Booz, Allen and Hamilton, (1982) *New Product Management for the 1980s,* Booz, Allen and Hamilton Consultants, New York.

Bosomworth, C.E. and Sage, Burton, H. Jr (1995) 'How 26 Companies Manage Their Central Research', *Research Technology Management,* May–June, 1995: 33–40.

Boulding, C. (1994) 'Are Surveys A Valuable Source Of Information, Or An Imprecise Discipline That Tells Marketers What They Want To Hear?', *Marketing Week,* 7 October, 1994, 36–39.

Bower, J.L. (1970) *Managing The Resource Allocation Process,* Homewood, Illinois.

British Standards Institute (1989) 'Guide to Managing Product Design', *BS7000,* BSI, London.

Brooksbank, R.W. (1991) 'Successful Marketing Practice: A Literature Review and Checklist for Marketing Practitioners', *European Journal of Marketing* **25** (5): 20–29.

Brown, A.D. and Ennew, C.T. (1995) 'Market Research and the Politics of New Product Development', *Journal of Marketing Management* 11: 339–353.

Brown, K. and Johnston, C. (1991) *Community Health Care,* Macmillan Magazines Ltd.

Brownlie, D. and Spender, J.C. (1995) 'Managerial Judgement in Strategic Marketing: Some Preliminary Thoughts,' *Management Decision* **33** (6): 39–50.

Bruce, M. and Biemans, W.G. (1995) *Product Development: Meeting the Challenge of the Design-Marketing Interface,* John Wiley & Sons, Chichester, UK.

Bruce, M. (1997) 'New Product Development' in D. A. Luther and B. Lewis (eds) *Dictionary of Marketing,* Blackwells, Oxford, UK.

Calabrese, G. (1997) 'Communication and Co-operation in Product Development. A Case Study of a European Car Producer', *R&D Management* **27** (3): 239–252.

Conway, H.A. and McGuinness, N.W. (1986) 'Idea Generation in Technology Based Firms', *Journal of Product Innovation Management* **1**: 276–291.

Coombs, R., Paviotti, P. and Walsh, V. (1987) *Economics and technological Change,* Rowman & Littefield Publishers, New York.

Coombs, R. (1998) 'A Reflection on the Major Themes of the 1997 R&D Management Conference,' *R&D Management* **28** (3): 213–214.

Cooper, R.G. (1979) 'Dimensions of Industrial New Product Success and Failure', *Journal of Marketing* **43**: 93–103.

Cooper, R.G. (1981) An Empirically Derived New Product Selection Model', *IEEE Transactions on Engineering Management* **EM-28** (3): 54–61.

Cooper, R.G. (1988) 'The New product Process: A decision guide for management', *Journal of Marketing Management* **3** (3): 238–255.

Cooper, R.G. (1993) *Winning at New Products: Accelerating the Process from Idea to Launch*, 2nd Edition, Addison-Wesley Publishing, Lexington, Mass.

Cooper, R.G. (1994) 'Third Generation New Product Processes', *Journal of Product Innovation Management* **11**: 3–14.

Cooper, R.G. and Jones, T. (1995) 'The Interfaces Between Design and other key functions in Product Development' in M. Bruce and W. Biemans (eds) *Product Development,* John Wiley & Sons, Chichester, UK.

Cooper, R. and Kleinschmidt, E.J. (1986) 'An Investigation in to the New Product Process: Steps, Deficiences and Impact', *Journal of Product Innovation Management* **3**: 71–85.

Cooper, R.G. and Kleinschmidt, E.J. (1987) 'Success Factors in Product Innovation', *Industrial Marketing Management* **16**: 215–223.

Cooper, R.G. and Kleinschmidt, E.J. (1988) 'New Products: What Separates Winners from Losers?', *Journal of Product Innovation Management* **4** (3): 169–184.

Cooper, R.G. and Kleinschmidt, E.J. (1988) 'Resource Allocation in the New Product Development process', *Industrial Marketing Management* **17**: 249–262.

Cooper, R.G. and Kleinschmidt, E.J. (1988) 'Success Factors in Product Innovation/, *Industrial Marketing Management* **16**: 215–223.

Cooper, R.G. and Kleinschmidt, E.J. (1993) 'Screening New Products for Potential Winners', *Long Range Planning* **26** (6): 74–81.

Computer Equipment Manufacturers (1996) Business Ratio Report, *Business Ratio*, London.

Crawford, C.M. (1987) *New Products Management,* Irwin, Homewood, USA.

Crawford, C.M. (1988) *New Products Management,* Irwin, Homewood, USA.

Daft, R. and Weick, K. (1984) 'Toward a Model of Organizations As Interpretation Systems', *Academy of Management Review* **9**: 284–295.

Davis, R.E. (1993) 'From Experience: The Role of Market research in the Development of New Consumer products', *Journal of product Innovation Management* **10**: 309–317.

De Bont, C.J.P.M. (1992) *Consumer Evaluations of Early product Concepts,* Delft University Press, Delft, Holland.

Design News (1993) 22 February, 1993: 25–26.

DTI (1995) *Learning from Japan,* DTI/Andersen Consulting, London, UK.

The Economist (1997) **344** (8034): S5(3).

Faulkner, Wendy (1994) 'Conceptualizing Knowledge Used in Innovation: A Second Look at the Science-Technology Distinction and Industrial Innovation'. *Science, Technology & Human Values* **19** (4): 425–458.

Feldman, L.P. and Page, A.L. (1984) 'Principles Versus Practice in New Product Planning', *Journal of Product Innovation Management* **1**: 43–55.

Financial Times (1996) *Financial Times*, 9 March, 1996.

Freeman, C. (1982) *The Economics of Industrial Innovation,* 2nd Edition, Frances Pinter, London.

Goldberg (1994).

Grammer, J. (1992) Lifecycle Management: Your Guide to Phase Reviews, GPT, Liverpool.

Grantham, L.M. (1997) 'The Validity of the Product Life Cycle in the High-Tech Industry', *Marketing Intelligence and Planning* **15** (1): 4–7.

Gupta, A.K., Rey, S.P. and Wileman, D. (1985) 'The R&D Marketing Interface in High-Technology Firms', *Journal of Product Innovation Management* **2**: 12–24.

Hamel, Gary and Prahalad, C.K. (1993) 'Strategy as Stretch and Leverage', *Harvard Business Review,* March–April, 1993: 75–85.

Hart, S. (1992) 'Dimensions of Success in NPD: An Exploratory Investigation', *Journal of Marketing Management* **9**: 23–41.

Hart, S. (1995) 'Where We've Been and Where We're Going in New Product Development Research', in M. Bruce and W.G. Biemans (eds) *Product Development: Meeting the Challenge of the Design-Marketing Interface,* John Wiley & Sons, Chichester, UK.

Hosley, S.M., Lau, A.T.W., Levy, F.K. and Tan, D.S.K. (1994) 'The Quest for the Competitive Learning Organization', *Management Decision* **32** (6): 5–15.

Iansiti, M. (1993) 'Real-World R&D: Jumping the Product Generation Gap', *Harvard Business Review,* May–June, 1993, 138–147.

Inkpen, A. (1995) 'The Seeking of Strategy Where it is not: Towards a Theory of Strategy Absence', *Strategic Management Journal* **16**: 313–323.

Ireland, C. and Johnson, B. (1995) 'Exploring the Future in the Present', *Design Management Journal,* Spring: 57–64.

Johne, A. and Snelson, P. (1988) 'Marketing's Role in Successful Product Development', *Journal of Marketing Management* **3** (3): 256–268.

Jones, T. (1997) *New Product Development: An Introduction to a Multifunctional Process,* Butterworth-Heinemann, Oxford.

Kinnear, T.C and Taylor, J.R. (1991) *Marketing Research: An Applied Approach,* 4th Edn, McGraw Hill, New York.

Kotler, P. (1980) *Principles of Marketing,* Prentice Hall, Englewood Cliffs, USA.

Kotler, P. (1988) *Marketing Management: Analysis, Planning, Implementation and Control,* 6th edition, Prentice Hall, Englewood Cliffs, USA.

Leonard-Barton, D. (1991) 'Inanimate Integrators: A Block of Wood Speaks', *Design Management International* **2** (3): 60–67.

Leonard-Barton, D. (1992) 'Core Capabilities and Core Rigidities: A Paradox in Managing New Product Development', *Strategic Management Journal* **13**: 111–125.

Leonard-Barton, D. (1995) 'Learning from the Market' in D. Leonard-Barton (ed.) *Wellsprings of Knowledge,* Harvard Business School Press, Boston, Mass.

Lowe, A. and Hunter, R.B. (1991) The *Role of Design and Marketing Management in the Culture of Innovation,* Proceedings of the European Marketing Academy Conference, Paris, France.

Mahoney, J.T. and Pandian, J.R. (1992) 'The Resource-Based View Within The Conversation of Strategic Management', *Strategic Management Journal* **13**: 363–380.

Marketing (1994) 'NPD: Getting the Priorities Right', *Marketing*, 10 November, 1994, 5.

Mathot, G.M.B. (1982) 'How to Get New products to Market Quicker', *Long Range Planning* **5** (6): 20–30.

McDonough E.F. III, and Leifer, R.P. (1986) 'Effective Control of New Product Projects: The Interaction of Organization Culture and Project Leadership', *Journal of Product Innovation Management* **3**: 149–157.

McKenzie, S. (1996) 'Best of Both Worlds: Qualitative and Quantitative Research is Essential for NPD: But Which Mix is Best?', *Marketing Week,* June 21, 1996: 61–67.

Meyers, P.W. (1990) Non-linear Learning in Large Technological Firms: Period four implies chaos. Research Policy 19: Urban et al. (1980)-115.

Meyers, P.W. and Wilemon, D. (1989) 'Learning in New Technology Development Teams', *Journal of Product Innovation Management* **6**: 79–88.

Meyers, S. and Marquis, D.G. (1989) 'Successful Industrial Innovation: A study of Factors Underlying Innovation in Selected Firms', *National Science Foundation Technology Report* **69** (17).

Mintzberg, H. (1975) 'The Manger's Job: Folklore and Fact', *Harvard Business Review* July/August: 163–176.

Mintzberg, H. and Quinn, J. (1991) *The Strategy Process: Concepts, Contexts, Courses,* 2nd edition, prentice Hall, Englewood Cliffs, USA.

Moenaert, R.K. and Souder, W.E. (1989) 'An Analysis of the Use of Extra-functional Information by R&D and Marketing Personnel: Review and Model', *Journal of Product Innovation Management* **7**: 213–229.

Moenaert, R.K. and Souder, W.E. (1990) 'An Analysis of the Use of Extra-functional Information by R&D and Marketing Personnel: Review and Model, *Journal of Product Innovation Management* **11**: 34–45.

Moore, W.I. and Pessemier, E.A. (1993) *Product Planning and Management: Designing and Delivering Value,* McGraw.

Myers, S. and Marquis, D. (1969) 'Successful Industrial Innovation', *National Science Foundation Technology Report* **69** (17).

Nishikawa, T. (1989) 'New Product Planning at Hitachi', *Long Range Planning* **22** (4): 20–24.

Nonaka, I. (1999) 'The Knowledge-Creating Company', *Harvard Business Review* Nov/Dec: 96–104.

Nystrom, H. (1979) *Creativity and Innovation,* John Wiley & Sons, Chichester, UK.

Page, A. and Stovall, J. (1994) *Importance of the Early Stages in the New Product Development process,* Proceedings of the 18th Annual PDMA International Conference on Bridging the Gap from Concept to Commercialisation, PDMA, USA.

Page, A.L. (1992) 'Assessing New Product Development Practices and Performance: Establishing Crucial Norms', *Journal of Product Innovation Management* **10**: 273-277.

Palframan, D. (1994) 'Concurrent Affairs', *Computing,* 2 June, 1994, 32.

Parnes, S.J. (1961) 'Effects of Extended Effort in Creative Problem-Solving', *Journal of Educational Psychology,* 52.

Pavia, M.T. (1992) 'The Early Stages of New Product Development in Entrepreneurial High Technology Firms', *Journal of Product Innovation Management* **8**: 18–31.

Pettigrew, A.M. (1973) *The Politics of Organisational Decision Making,* Tavistock, London.

Pettigrew, A. and Whipp, R. (1991) *Managing Change for Competitive Success,* Blackwell, Oxford.

Piercy, N. (1989) 'Marketing Concepts and Actions: Implementing Marketing-led Strategic Change', *European Journal of Marketing* **24** (2): 24–39.

Pinto, M. and Pinto, J.K. (1990) 'Project Team Communication and Cross-Functional Cooperation in New Program Development', *Journal of Product Innovation Management* **7**: 200–212.

Power, C. (1993) 'Flops: Too Many New Products Fail: Here's Why and How To Do Better', *Business Week,* 16 August, 1993.

Prahalad, C.K. and Hamel, G. (1990) 'The Role of Core Competencies in the Corporation,' *Harvard Business Review,* May–June, 1990, 79–91.

Prahalad, C.K. and Hamel, G. (1991) 'Corporate Imagination and Expeditionary Marketing', *Harvard Business review,* July-August, 1991, 81–92.

Quinn, J.B., Mintzberg, H. and James, M.R. (1988) *The Strategy Process-Concepts, Contexts and Cases,* Prentice Hall, New York.

Rainey, J. (1995) *The Effects of Marketing strategies on Community Nurses Selection of Wound Dressings,* Proceedings of the 5th European Conference on Advances in Wound Management, 21–24 November, 1995, Harrogate, UK.

Ranganath Nayak, P. and Ketteringham, J.M. (1987) *Breakthroughs,* Mercury Books, W.H. Allen & Co., New York.

Rickards, T. and Moger, S. (1999) *Handbook for Creative Team Leaders,* Gower, Aldershot, UK.

Rickards, T. (1991) 'Innovation and Creativity: Woods, Trees and Pathways, *R&D Management* **21** (2): 97–108.

Roberts, A. (1996) *Market Research Tools and Techniques for the 'Front End' of Product Development,* UMIST, Manchester, UK.

Rochford, L. (1991) 'Generating and Screening New Product Ideas', *Industrial Marketing Management* **20**: 287–296.

Rochford, L. and Rudelius, W. (1992) 'How Involving More Functional Areas Within a Firm Affects the New Product Process. *Journal of Product Innovation Management* **9**: 287–299.

Root-Bernstein, R.S. (1989) 'Who Discovers and Invents', *Research Technology Management,* January–February, 1989.

Rothwell, R. (1992) 'Developments Towards the Fifth Generation Model of Innovation', *Technology Analysis & Strategic Management* **1** (4): 73–75.

Schilling, M.A. and Hill, C.W.L. (1998) 'Managing the New Product Development Process: Strategic Imperatives', *The Academy of Management Executives* **12** (3): 67.

Sheridan, J.H. (1998) 'Companies Emphasise Product Innovation', *Industry Week* **247** (9): 13.

Sheridan, J.H. (1998) 'Nurturing Successful Innovation', *Industry Week* **247** (10): 16.

Sobek, D.K. II, Liker, J.K. and Ward, A.C. (1998) 'Another Look at how Toyota Integrates New Product Development', *Harvard Business Review* **76** (4): 36.

Souder, W.E. (1998) 'Managing Relations between R&D and Marketing in New Internet Development Projects', *Journal of Product Innovation Management* **5**: 6–19.

Sowrey, T. (1989) 'Idea Generation: Identifying the Most Useful Techniques', *European Journal of Marketing* **24** (5): 20–29.

Stalk, G., Evans, P. and Shulman, L.E. (1992) 'Competing on Capabilities: The New Rules of Corporate Strategy', *Harvard Business Review,* March–April, 1992: 57–69.

Takeuchi, H. and Nonaka, I. (1986) 'The New Conduct Development Game', *Harvard Business Review* Jan/Feb: 137–146.

Tersine, R.J. and Hummingbird, E.A. (1995) 'Lead-Time Reduction: The Search for Competitive Advantage', *International Journal of Operations and Production Management* **15** (2): 8–19.

Tidd, J. (1993) 'Technological Innovation, Organizational Linkages and Strategic Degrees of Freedom', *Technology Analysis & Strategic Management* **5** (3): 273–284.

Tidd, J., Bessant, J. and Pavitt, K. (1997) *Managing Innovation: Integrating Technological, Market and Organisational Change,* John Wiley & Sons, Chichester, UK.

Ulrich, K.T. and Eppinger, S.D. (1995) *Product Design and Development*, McGraw Hill, New York.

Urban, G.L. and Hauser, J.R. (1980) *Design and Marketing of New Products*, Prentice Hall, Englewood Cliffs, USA and UK.

Utterback, J.M. (1974) 'Innovation in Industry and the Diffusion of Technology', *Science* **183** (15 February): 658–662.

Van de Ven, A.H. (1986) 'Central Problems in the Management of Innovation', *Management Science* **32** (5): 590–607.

Van de Ven, A.H. and Walker, G. (1984) 'The Dynamics of Inter-organizational Coordination,' *Administrative Science Quarterly* **29**: 598–621.

Verganti, R. (1997) 'Leveraging on Systematic Learning to Manage the Early Phases of Product Innovation Projects', *R&D Management* **27** (4): 377–392.

Von Hippel, E. (1978) 'Successful Industrial Products From Customer Ideas', *Journal of Marketing* **42** (1): 39–49.

Vowden, K.R., Barker, A. and Vowden, P. (1996) *Experience of a Nurse-Led, Hospital Based Leg Ulcer Clinic*, Proceedings of the 6th European Conference on Advances in Wound management, 1–4 October, 1996, Amsterdam.

Walsh, V., Roy, R., Bruce, M. and Potter, S. (1992) *Winning by Design: Technology, Product, Design and International Competitiveness*, Blackwell, Oxford.

Wang, Q. (1997) 'R&D/Marketing Interface in a Firm's Capability-Building Process: Evidence from Pharmaceutical Firms', *International Journal of Innovation Management* **1** (1): 23–52.

Webster, C. (1993) 'Refinement of the Marketing Culture Scale and the Relationship Between Marketing Culture and the Profitability of a Service Firm', *Journal of Business Research* **26**, 111–131.

Whelan, R.C. (1988) How To Prioritize R&D. R & D Management Conference Paper, Manchester Business School, Manchester, UK.

Wilson, D.T. and Ghingold, M. (1987) 'Linking R&D to Market Needs', *Industrial Marketing Management* **6**: 207–214.

Wind, Y.J. (1982) *Product Policy: Concept Methods of Strategy*, Addison Wesley, Lexington, Mass.

Wind, J. and Mahajan, V. (1997) 'Issues and Opportunities in New Product Development: An Introduction to the Special Issue', *Journal of Marketing Research* **XXXIV** (February): 1–12.

Woudhuysen, J. (1994) 'Tailoring IT to the Needs of Customers', *Long Range Planning* **27** (3): 33–42.

Zabriskie, N.B. and Huellmantel, A.B. (1994) 'Marketing Research as a Strategic Tool', *Long Range Planning* **27** (1): 107–118.

INDEX